Contents

4.75N

The Evaluation of an
Intervention Programme
for Disadvantaged Children

WITHDRAWN

Thomas Kellaghan

NFER Publishing

N 0004511 X

Published by the NFER Publishing Company Ltd.,
2 Jennings Buildings, Thames Avenue,
Windsor, Berks. SL4 1QS
Registered Office: The Mere, Upton Park, Slough, Berks. SL1 2DQ
First published 1977
© Thomas Kellaghan, 1977
ISBN 085633 124 4

Printed in Great Britain by
Staples Printers, Love Lane, Rochester, Kent
Distributed in the USA by Humanities Press Inc.,
Atlantic Highlands, New Jersey 07716 USA.

INTRODUCTION

The problem of children in areas that have come to be known as 'disadvantaged' came sharply into focus in the 1960s. Broadly speaking, these areas were sections of cities with a heavy concentration of poor housing, a high proportion of unskilled and unemployed workers and a high rate of educational failure. The problem, of course, was not new, but efforts to cope with it were. Particularly in the United States, a vast amount of money and human resources was thrown into its solution. These efforts involved detailed studies of disadvantaged areas as well as of the characteristics of children living in them. But for the most part, they involved the development of programmes to help children from disadvantaged backgrounds at various stages during their educational careers.

Interest in the problems of the disadvantaged, and in the search for possible approaches to deal with them, developed in Europe in the late 1960s; at an early stage, an active interest in the problems was shown in Ireland. In 1967, a committee on educational retardation established by the Minister for Education recommended special arrangements for schools in culturally disadvantaged areas and a number of proposals for special intervention were considered. In 1968, an opportunity presented itself to set up, on an experimental basis, a programme for children in a disadvantaged area of central Dublin, which had a history of high educational failure. The Bernard Van Leer Foundation indicated its willingness to cooperate with the Department of Education in the funding of such a project. In planning the project, two main points were borne in mind. The first was that in view of the marked relationship between measured intelligence at the pre-school stage and at maturity, early intervention was desirable. The second was that since the child's home was the main formative influence in the early years, the active involvement of parents in the educational process should be sought. The result of these concerns was the establishment of a pre-school for children aged between three and five years, with the major aim of assisting in the development of the cognitive skills of the children and, by so doing, to prepare them for the work of the primary school. Since a curriculum for three-year-old children did not exist in Irish national schools, it was necessary to develop one for the project. This was done during the first year of the project and continued through its second year when the children were four years of age. After completing two years in the pre-school, children could transfer to an adjacent junior primary school for a further period of three years. Attempts were made to adapt the junior school curriculum to the needs of the children, but these attempts were less intensive than at the pre-school level. Not all children transferred to the junior school, some choosing instead to go to other schools.

At the inception of the project, provision was made for its evaluation. Basically there were two aspects to this. The first was to trace the development of the children over a five year period. The second involved comparing characteristics of the children who had participated in the pre-school programme with characteristics of a group of similar children who had not participated in such a programme. The choice of the group of 'similar' or control children caused many problems. Eventually, it was decided to take a group of children living in the area who were aged eight at the inception of the project. The performance of the experimental group, on reaching the age of eight, would be compared with the performance of this group.

The author of this report was responsible for the evaluation of the project. Obviously, he did not carry it out single-handed. All involved in the project — director, teachers, testers and social workers — assisted in every possible way at all stages of the evaluation. Teachers in other schools also provided facilities for testing and information on the progress of children while parents were most helpful and cooperative in supplying information in interviews. For assistance in the collection of data, the author is indebted to Dr Betty Jane Greaney, Elizabeth Neuman, Deirdre Brugha and Joy O'Reilly. Dr Greaney also carried out the major analyses for the evaluation and wrote the survey of parents' reactions to the programme (Chapter VII). Other people provided assistance either during the developmental stage of the project or during its evaluation. The author wishes to express his gratitude particularly to Tomas O'Cuilleanain and Tomas Gilin, Department of Education, Dublin; to Dr W.H. Welling, Dr A.W. Wood and Dr F. Kessel of the Van Leer Foundation, The Hague; to Dr Vincent Greaney, Dr George Madaus, Dr Patricia Fontes, Michael Martin and Paul Kelly all of the Educational Research Centre, St Patrick's College, Dublin; to the interviewers and testers; to Dr D.F. Cregan, Simon Clyne and Mrs Carmel Finn, St Patrick's College, Dublin; to Dr Ira Gordon, University of Florida; to Dr David Weikart, High / Scope Educational Research Foundation, Ypsilanti, Michigan; to Dr A.H. Passow and Dr Helen Robinson, Columbia University; to Dr James A. Wilson and Dr O.K. Moore, University of Pittsburgh; and to Dr Corinne Mumbauer, George Peabody College for Teachers, Nashville, Tennessee.

I am particularly indebted to Seamus Holland, Director of the project for his unfailing assistance and support throughout the life of the project. He also provided material for Chapter III in this report.

The financial assistance of the Department of Education and the Van Leer Foundation, without which the project or the evaluation would not have been possible, is also acknowledged.

Finally, I am indebted to Mary Rohan, Patricia Kingston, Jane Kelly, Karl McGee and Siobhan Simmons for assistance in the preparation of the manuscript. Mary Rohan, as well as providing bibliographic assistance and preparing tables and figures, also typed the manuscript with the assistance of Patricia Kingston.

TK

Chapter I

The Disadvantaged

A cursory glance at the history of education indicates that particular problems come into focus at different times. Thus, for example, at different periods, the problems of the mentally handicapped, those of the physically handicapped and, more recently, problems of the disadvantaged have each been the focus of attention. The fact that a problem does not receive widespread and public attention does not, of course, mean that it does not exist. Problems of children who have difficulty in acquiring basic scholastic skills — for whatever reason — are perennially present to teachers, whether or not such problems are the concern of policy makers and whether or not they receive the attention of specialists. In almost every class, one is likely to come across at least a few children who have great difficulty in acquiring one or more of the basic skills — reading, writing, spelling or numerical computation. In some cases, the number may be much larger; a school in a poor neighbourhood or the lowest stream in a tracked system may contain many children with a learning problem. No doubt, teachers learn to cope with such situations, one way or another, and with varying degrees of success (Kellaghan, 1976a).

During the past fifteen years, the problem of a group of children who have come to be known as disadvantaged has been receiving increasing attention from educators, policy makers, administrators and researchers in education, and efforts have been made to supplement teachers' resources in dealing with the problem. A variety of terms has been used to label more or less the same phenomena. Riessman (1962) admits to using interchangeably through his book *The Culturally Deprived Child* the terms 'culturally deprived', 'educationally deprived', 'underprivileged', 'lower class' and 'lower socioeconomic group'; other terms that have been used are 'socially disadvantaged', 'inner city' or 'ghetto child' (Passow and Elliott, 1968).

The complexity of the condition of disadvantage and the terms themselves suggest a number of different frames of reference —

economic, educational, cultural and social — from which the condition may be viewed. An attempt to standardize terminology was made at a UNESCO meeting on deprivation and disadvantage in Hamburg in 1967. Since the term and the definition which were agreed upon at this meeting are both comprehensive and concise, as well as being particularly relevant to education, they seem appropriate in the context of a study of pre-schooling and will be used here. According to the definition, a child may be regarded as disadvantaged if, because of socio-cultural reasons, he comes into the school system with knowledge, skills and attitudes which make adjustment difficult and impede learning (Passow, 1970). There are three aspects to the definition. The first refers to the personal characteristics of the child. The knowledge, skills and attitudes he brings with him to school are, by implication, different from those which most children bring. By knowledge is meant such things as store of information and range of vocabulary. Skills may refer to perceptual ones (e.g., the ability to analyse a geometric figure) or higher cognitive ones (e.g., the ability to organize and categorize experience) or skills of language (e.g., the ability to string sentences together, to listen to a story and repeat the main points in the given sequence). Attitudes too can refer to a wide variety of phenomena — to knowledge, to learning, to books, to sitting down and staying quiet. The second aspect of the definition points to the child's background. His knowledge, skills and attitudes are the result of living in a particular kind of material and socio-cultural environment. The disadvantaged home differs from the middle class one in its material conditions, in its authority structure, in attitudes to learning and to exploring the environment and in its language models. It is in adjusting to this kind of environment that the peculiar knowledge, skills and attitudes of the disadvantaged child develop in the first place. The third aspect of the definition refers to the educational demands which will be made on the child. The child's skills, knowledge and attitudes are not in harmony with those demanded by the school, and so, learning does not proceed at the rate at which it does — to make a comparison — in the case of the middle class child. It has been argued that not only do disadvantaged children start school with a disadvantage but, as they move through the classes, the gap in scholastic attainment between them and middle class children increasingly widens (Deutsch, 1963). The overall effect is that disadvantaged children are 'unable to participate fully in that cultural heritage which the school transmits' and so 'are deprived of part of their cultural inheritance' (Moss, 1973, p. 20).

Related concepts

Problems associated with being disadvantaged are by no means new. Although the term itself came into general use only in the 1960s, many notions associated with disadvantage had long been recognized. Of particular relevance are the concept of poverty and the relationship between scholastic aptitude and attainment on the one hand and environmental factors (particularly home factors) on the other.

Poverty is a condition which apparently always existed, but it assumes new dimensions in an industrial urbanized society. In modern society, the contrast between lack of material goods and affluence becomes more pronounced; besides, in an industrial setting, the poor lack the basic resources and control they would possess in a rural environment, even if living at a subsistence level. Poverty is frequently defined in terms of limitation of income, though other criteria have also been used, such as community resources (e.g., limited employment opportunities), personal characteristics (such as age, level of education and skill that may affect a person's chances in the labour market) and behavioural or attitudinal characteristics that set poor people off from other groups in society (Ferman, Kornbluh and Haber, 1965).

Several kinds of poverty have been identified (Social Science Research Council, 1968); of most concern to us is the 'down-town' variety. This kind of poverty is geographically concentrated; areas characterized by poor housing conditions, over-crowding and low income are a feature of most large cities. To what extent the poverty existing in these areas is situational (Duncan, 1969) or cultural (Lewis, 1969) is a question of debate. According to the situational approach, the poor are primarily different because of their low income, which limits what they can do. The cultural approach on the other hand sees the poor, as a response to economic privation and uncertainty, as having developed a subculture of beliefs, values and behavioural traits which set them off from the affluent groups in a society. The culture is seen as being passed on from one generation to the next. How one views poverty has implications for treatment or intervention. If poverty is viewed as basically situational, then treatment is likely to focus on employment policies and the redistribution of income. If, on the other hand, poverty is seen as basically cultural, treatment is more likely to focus on community action, social work and education. Halsey (1972) points out that American action to deal with poverty in the 1960s (particularly the Economic Opportunity Act of 1964), which focussed on community and educational change, was based on a cultural view of poverty. However, urban industrial poverty more likely possesses both situational and cultural characteristics and so proposed solutions should involve economic as well as cultural reform.

While many children from poor homes would be regarded as disadvantaged in the school situation, poverty and disadvantage are not coterminous. Some children from materially poor homes are not disadvantaged as far as their knowledge, skills and attitudes in the school situation are concerned. Increasing stress is being placed on the heterogeneity among populations which exist in areas that appear conducive to the development of conditions of disadvantage (E. Gordon, 1970). On the other hand, a child from a well-off home also may be disadvantaged in that his value system may conflict with that of the school (Fantini and Weinstein, 1968). By and large, however, skills and values fostered in a middle class home are more likely to be congruent with those of the school than the skills and values fostered in a very poor home.

In investigating the relationship between environmental factors on the one hand and scholastic aptitude and attainment on the other, social class membership has been the environmental factor most frequently considered. Measures of scholastic aptitude and attainment have included intelligence tests, standardized attainment tests and retention in the educational system. The relationship between social class on the one hand and scholastic aptitude and attainment on the other is one of the best documented in the field of educational inquiry. Ever since the time of Binet, it has been recognized that intelligence test scores and school performance both rise with social level. In Ireland, the relationships have recently been empirically documented. A positive relationship between verbal reasoning ability and social class has been reported for a national sample of eleven-year-old children (Kellaghan and Macnamara, 1972) while a study of a more restricted sample found that educational retardation is also associated with social class (Cullen, 1969).

Terms like social class and socioeconomic status are at best descriptive; they certainly are not explanatory. At least nineteen indices of social class have been used — among them, occupation, family income and educational level. Since all are highly interrelated, they presumably measure the same underlying dimensions (Kahl and Davis, 1955). However, the question remains: what are the factors associated with social class that affect scholastic behaviour and how do they operate? How does father's occupational level or amount of wealth get translated into meaningful educational variables?

There have been many attempts to elucidate how particular factors, events or processes in the child's home affect cognitive processes and scholastic progress (*cf.* Marjoribanks, 1974a, 1974b). The material level of the home (income and space) has been considered (Fraser, 1959); so have more cultural aspects, such as parents' educational level, home literacy, reading habits and language behaviour (Dave, 1963; Fraser, 1959; Milner, 1949; Peaker, 1967; Van Alstyne, 1929; Wiseman, 1967; Wolf, 1964). Attitudinal and motivational factors have also been found to be related to scholastic progress (Dave, 1963; Floud, Halsey and Martin, 1957; Fraser, 1959; Freeburg and Payne, 1967; Great Britain:

Department of Education and Science, 1967; Peaker, 1967; Wiseman, 1967).

The development of interest in the disadvantaged has led to an increased interest in the study of home variables and their relationship to cognitive development. Early socialization processes, the teaching style and control techniques of mothers and their attitudes towards child-rearing have all received attention (Hess and Shipman, 1965, 1967; Kagan, 1969; Olim, Hess and Shipman, 1967; Radin and Kamii, 1965; Zigler, 1970). These are areas of investigation which promise to throw considerable light on the dynamics of development in a disadvantaged background. So far, the evidence suggests that a wide range of home variables can influence the development of the child. The general learning opportunities provided by the home seem of central importance (e.g., opportunities for thinking and planning in daily activities, the use of books, periodicals and library facilities); so too do parental pressures, expressed in parents' aspirations for the child and the kinds of rewards they give for intellectual development. These findings have been interpreted as indicating the feasibility of effecting changes in the cognitive growth of children through changes in their home environments. With evidence of correlations as high as .76 between home factors and intelligence (Wolf, 1964), the ramifications of modifying home environments seem significant. On this basis, several home intervention programmes for children in disadvantaged backgrounds have already been undertaken (*cf.* I.J. Gordon, 1971, 1973, 1975; Kellaghan and Archer, 1973).

Characteristics of the disadvantaged

Efforts to identify disadvantaged children have involved attempts to render more explicit the criteria outlined in the definition of disadvantage we considered above. Both the environmental and personal aspects of disadvantage have received considerable attention. The environmental approach has focussed both on geographical areas and on home conditions. Descriptions of disadvantage in terms of home conditions have most frequently focussed on status variables, such as socioeconomic class, income, occupation and size of family. Other descriptions have concerned themselves more with the dynamics of family life: spatial and temporal disorganization in the home (Klaus and Gray, 1968); the matrifocal character of the family (Halsey, 1972); limitations in the interaction of parents and children (Hunt, 1969; Kagan, 1969; Radin and Kamii, 1965); the tendency of the home to be status-oriented rather than person-oriented and the consequences of this tendency for the control of behaviour (Hess and Shipman, 1965); and the use and functions of language in the home (Bernstein, 1960, 1961, 1971; Hess and Shipman, 1965, 1967; Olim, Hess and Shipman,

1967). All these areas raise interesting topics for investigation; however, knowledge relating to any of the topics is not sufficiently developed to make any strong generalizations about the characteristics of disadvantaged homes.

Since homes that share the above characteristics are often concentrated in particular geographical areas (*cf.* Burt, 1937), attempts have been made to establish criteria for the identification of such areas. The Plowden Report (Great Britain: Department of Education and Science, 1967) advanced eight criteria for the identification of what the report called educational priority areas: social class composition, size of families, supplements in cash or kind from the state, over-crowding, poor school attendance, proportions of retarded, disturbed or handicapped pupils, incomplete families and children unable to speak English. Three further criteria were later added: poor or inadequate housing, high pupil turnover and high teacher turnover. In practice, the Plowden formula suffers from certain disadvantages. The relationship between home background or demographic measures on the one hand and the actual scholastic progress of children on the other is far from perfect. One has to be cautious, on the basis of the area in which children live, about the disadvantages they may suffer. Poor scholastic progress and learning difficulties are by no means limited to the kind of areas which the Plowden approach would identify. On the basis of analyses carried out in educational priority areas, it was concluded that 'it seems likely that the majority of disadvantaged children are not in disadvantaged areas, and the majority of children in disadvantaged areas are not disadvantaged' (Barnes, 1975, p. 248). The identification of educational priority areas, then, can only be regarded as a first step in the identification of the disadvantaged child (Chazan, Laing and Jackson, 1971).

To overcome this problem, the California Advisory Committee on Compensatory Education used a combination of personal and environmental characteristics in their list of criteria of disadvantage. According to the Committee, children are disadvantaged if they are below average in school achievement as measured by standardized tests in combination with one or more of the following problems: economic deprivation, social alienation caused by racial or ethnic discrimination and geographic isolation.

The most obvious personal characteristic associated with disadvantage, as indicated by the California Advisory Committee's criteria, is poor scholastic progress. This may be manifested in poor scholastic aptitude, poor attainment in school subjects or in early school leaving. It was, in fact, factors such as these that focussed attention on the problem of the disadvantaged in the first place. A recent approach to the identification of the disadvantaged in the State of Michigan recommended scholastic attainment as the sole criterion for receiving additional financial aid. According to the Michigan Plan, state funds for compensatory education would be allocated on the basis of the number of pupils in elementary school (K—6) who are found to be in need of 'substantial improvement' in the basic skills of reading and / or arithmetic. Pupils scoring below the 15th percentile on a state-wide testing programme qualify for assistance (Madaus and Elmer, 1973). The Quie Bill in the United States Senate also proposed the use of a measure of scholastic attainment to estimate the number of educationally disadvantaged children in each state of the union; the measure proposed, however, was a criterion-referenced test, not a norm-referenced one as used in Michigan (Madaus and Elmore, 1973).

Apart from scholastic progress, a host of other variables have been investigated in the context of disadvantage. Differences between disadvantaged and other children have been reported in perceptual (auditory and visual) development (Passow and Elliott, 1967) as well as in the development of higher cognitive functions. For example, disadvantaged children have been described as more motoric than conceptual in their orientation (Gans, 1962; J.E. Gordon, 1968; Passow and Elliott, 1967). Jensen (1972, 1973) has argued that higher cognitive ability involving complex operations and transformational processes (level 11 ability) is less well developed in disadvantaged children than lower level associative ability (level 1 ability).

The development of language in the disadvantaged has received a great deal of attention (Cazden, 1966; Deutsch, 1963; Jensen, 1967, 1968; Krauss and Rotter, 1968). Earlier views, particularly those associated with Bernstein (1960, 1961), which emphasized the restricted nature of the language of the disadvantaged, have been the subject of close examination and no longer seem tenable (Bernstein, 1971; Edwards, 1974; Jones and McMillan, 1973; Labov, 1969, 1972). The study of defects has now largely given way to the study of differences (Kessel, 1974). Furthermore, in studying differences, more attention is now given to differences between groups in language usage than in language structure (Cazden, John and Hymes, 1972; Halliday, 1973; Tough, 1973a, 1973b).

In the area of personality, motivation and interpersonal relations, many efforts have also been made to portray differences between disadvantaged and other children. These efforts related to the ability to delay gratification (Kluckhohn and Strodtbeck, 1961; Miller, Riessman and Seagull, 1965; Mischel, 1961), the ability to feel guilt (J.E. Gordon, 1968), aggression (J.E. Gordon, 1968), self-concept (Ausubel and Ausubel, 1963; Deutsch, 1963, 1967), motivation (Deutsch, 1967; Henry, 1971; Passow and Elliott, 1967) and attentional difficulties

(Chazan, 1973).

The literature on personality characteristics of the disadvantaged has not all been negative. The strengths of the disadvantaged home have been noted and the cooperativeness and the lack of extreme competitiveness which such homes foster have been illustrated. The problems with which the disadvantaged are confronted, in the school and in the more general society in which they live, have also received attention and it has been pointed out that the school failure of many children from disadvantaged backgrounds cannot be divorced from problems which have their origin outside the world of the disadvantaged (Fantini, 1969; Tulkin, 1972). Finally, the danger of confusing differences with defects — particularly in the area of language — has been pointed out with increasing emphasis (Eisenberg, 1963; Ginsburg, 1972; Torrance, 1974).

We are still without satisfactory descriptions and measures of the personal characteristics of children in disadvantaged backgrounds. We are also still without adequate descriptions or measures of those backgrounds. And perhaps, of even greater importance, too many studies have adopted a normative approach in which the characteristics of disadvantaged children are compared to those of other children. There is a great need for studies in the tradition of Ruth Benedict (1934) which will examine and attempt to understand the 'patterns' of disadvantaged cultures.

So far, we are clear that children from backgrounds that we can describe in fairly general terms as disadvantaged can experience great difficulties in school. But not all children from such backgrounds experience such difficulties, and for those that do, it would be false to assume that the source of the difficulties lies exclusively in the deficiencies of the children themselves and of their backgrounds. For this reason, the very notion of compensation for disadvantaged children has been questioned (Sroufe, 1970): unless it is assumed that children have some kind of deficit, compensation does not seem an appropriate procedure. However, with the abundant evidence that is available concerning the school failure of children from particular kinds of background, it seems reasonable to take some action to assist such children in adapting to the work of the school. This does not necessarily imply a 'deficit' model. On the basis of a 'difference' model, one is not precluded from providing special means to help a child function in two types of environment or subculture — his own and that of the school. Neither is it implied that the onus of change must rest solely on the individual child. To help bring about desired changes in the child, it may also be necessary for the school to change, and some commentators (cf. Stanley, 1973) have expressed pessimism about existing efforts to deal with the problems of the disadvantaged, stressing instead the need for a fairly radical reorganization of school services. Perhaps when schools and those who work in them have been exposed to the same amount of investigation as the disadvantaged have, we will be in a better position to match the potentialities and needs of both.

Development of interest in the disadvantaged

Interest in the problems of the disadvantaged developed as a result of a variety of movements, philosophies and ideas that came to the fore in American society in the 1950s and 1960s. The development of interest in European countries seems to have been an overflow from the United States. It was probably largely mediated through the literature and through various international bodies like UNESCO, OECD and more recently the Council of Europe. However, it is unlikely that the American work would have evoked a response in Europe if the phenomena which the work dealt with were not perceived as being very real. And, of course, considerable research relating to disadvantage had already been carried out in Europe — research on poverty, on learning problems and on the relationship between home environment and school progress. More recently, the recognition of problems associated with disadvantage has led to studies in countries outside the United States and Europe (e.g., McKay, McKay and Sinisterra, 1973).

Some of the impetus in the United States came from the launching of Sputnik, when Russia moved ahead of America in the space race. Americans began to look critically at their schools. Among other things, they found that many science curricula were out of date; they also noted the poor attainment and early school drop-out of children from working class homes. The question arose: was a large amount of potential talent being lost to the nation? Interest in the disadvantaged as a particular group needing assistance, it was hoped, would help to ensure that the potential and resources of all children would be developed.

During the 1960s, the rise of the Civil Rights movement also contributed towards the development of interest in the disadvantaged. The pressure of this movement for better housing, better jobs, better education and better opportunities for the poor was a factor in the development of programmes to deal with the problems of the disadvantaged in the field of education (Ferman, Kornbluh and Haber, 1965).

Perhaps the major principle behind the development of programmes for the disadvantaged — at any rate, it is the one most frequently and explicitly stated — is the principle of equality of educational opportunity. The principle is one which is accepted in most democratic countries. At its simplest it means that all children — irrespective of such irrelevant criteria as creed, class, colour, sex, financial resources, or place of residence — should have equal access to educational facilities. In practice, it is difficult to determine whether or not such access is equally available to all sections of the community, since access is something that can be affected by factors more subtle and elusive than financial resources or even social class membership. A number of things are, however, clear. First, not all sections of the community participate to the same extent in the educational system. Secondly, the measured attainment of children in the system is related to their social class membership. And thirdly, post-school careers are also related to initial social class membership (*cf.* Coleman *et al.*, 1966; Husen, 1969; Investment in Education, 1966; Ireland: Central Statistics Office, 1970; Jencks *et al.*, 1972; Kellaghan and Greaney, 1970).

In a society such as ours that aspires to democratic and egalitarian ideals, the fact that one's educational and life chances are related to the social class membership of one's family is a cause of some discomfort. Various attempts have been made to improve the situation. These have included the system of selection introduced in the 1944 Education Act in Britain and, in Ireland, the provision of free post-primary education, the granting of scholarships and the raising of the school-leaving age. The success of such measures in influencing participation rates of different social groups in education, however, seems to be limited. It is now realized that the promotion of equal access in itself does not necessarily result in equality of participation.

It thus became apparent that it is not sufficient simply to provide identical educational treatment for all children, regardless of differences in aptitude, attainment and background, in the hope that all will derive reasonable benefit. Some children come to school well prepared to partake in the activities of the school; others, because they come from homes with different facilities, expectations and values, are poorly prepared for the work of the school. Providing these latter children with normal educational treatment will make for unequal rather than equal opportunity. Thus, it is argued, equality of opportunity demands differential treatment if one is to compensate for past deprivations in the case of those poorly prepared (Passow, 1970; Sussman, 1967). Such a view of equality is active rather than passive, demanding different school treatments for different kinds of children (Coleman, 1968).

The idea of differential treatment related to the needs of different sections of the community received political expression in the United States with the setting up of the Head Start, Title I and Upward Bound programmes as part of the war on poverty legislation of 1965. The same idea was embodied in the setting up of Educational Priority Areas in Britain in 1967. Both the American and British programmes were designed to deal with a particularly intractable educational problem, that of children in economically poor areas, for whom in the past the school has not served as a vehicle of social mobility.

Interest in the problems of the disadvantaged developed in Ireland in the 1960s. The Commission on Mental Handicap which reported in 1966 touched on the problems of the disadvantaged when it recommended the establishment of pre-school centres which would provide learning opportunities absent from their normal environment 'for children from areas where there is a concentration of families in the low income group' (Ireland: Commission of Inquiry on Mental Handicap, 1966, p. 123). In the 1960s also, the phenomenon of school failure was beginning to attract public attention. Research reports on standards in reading in the country (Kelly and McGee, 1967; Macnamara, 1966) probably contributed to this. By comparison with some other countries, Irish problems of disadvantage might appear slight: the country has no minority ethnic or racial groups, no immigration, and primary education has been available to the whole population for over a hundred years. Nevertheless, in the light of estimates in other countries, it is probably reasonable to assume that five per cent of the population of school-going children is disadvantaged; at the primary level that is approximately 25,000 children (Kellaghan, 1970).

The problem then is not insignificant, and several actions have been taken in recent years to explore it and seek solutions to it. These have included a number of studies of the characteristics of children in disadvantaged areas (Brugha, 1971; Carney, 1970; Chamberlain, 1970; McGee, 1970). The most significant action has been the establishment of an experimental pre-school centre which caters for three- and four-year-old children in a disadvantaged area in central Dublin (Kellaghan, 1971; Kellaghan and O'hUallachain, 1969, 1973). Further information about this project is provided in Chapter III.

Chapter II

Pre-school
Intervention Programmes

Attempts to deal with the problems of the disadvantaged have taken many forms and have focussed on different periods of the life cycle, from infancy to adulthood (*cf.* Passow, 1970). However, more resources have been put into the pre-school period than into any other. This perhaps was because of a current emphasis on the flexibility of development in the early years as well as the belief that critical periods of learning may exist early in life; both of these considerations received support in the work of psychologists and ethologists (Kellaghan, 1972).

The speed with which special educational programmes were launched in the United States, and the massiveness of their scale, was a source of admiration and optimism. However, the situation was all too soon to turn to one of criticism and pessimism (Thirion, 1974). It did not take long to find out that the basic knowledge on which to build a technology of intervention was not equal to the task. It is only during the last few years that the basic dimensions of that knowledge have begun to take shape.

Historically, intervention procedures in the United States may be categorized under two headings (McDill, McDill, and Sprehe, 1969). In the first category, there were three primarily administrative agencies (Head Start, Title I and Upward Bound) which grew out of the war on poverty legislation of the Johnson Administration in 1965. And secondly, there was a category of more independent local attempts at compensatory education throughout the country. Several of these were already in existence before the launching of Head Start. For example, the Early Training Project at George Peabody College in Nashville, Tennessee began in 1959 (*cf.* Klaus and Gray, 1968), the Perry Preschool Project at Ypsilanti, Michigan began in 1962 (*cf.* Weikart, 1967; Weikart, Deloria, Lawser and Wiegerink, 1970), and the programmes of the Institute for Developmental Studies in New York City began in 1958 (Deutsch, 1963). Great variations existed between local programmes in their size, in cost, and in intensity, type and length of treatment (McDill, McDill and Sprehe, 1972). Many of them were associated with academic institutions, which probably meant that planning and evaluation aspects of the programmes received more attention than in Head Start.

Of the administrative agencies (*cf*. Gordon and Wilkerson, 1966; Havighurst, 1970; Little and Smith, 1971; McDill, McDill and Sprehe, 1969, 1972), the largest concerned Head Start, an intervention programme for pre-schoolers, which had as its aim the preparation for the ordinary school of children from disadvantaged backgrounds. Initially, the programme was of eight weeks' duration in the summer, and during its first year of operation (1965), over 500,000 children took part. At the end of the summer, an additional one-year programme was provided for some children. By 1969, the programme was reaching 650,000 children, of whom 214,000 were in the full-year programme, at a cost of $330 million per year (McDill, McDill and Sprehe, 1972). The other agencies, Title I of the Elementary and Secondary Education Act and Upward Bound were concerned mainly with elementary and pre-college students respectively. The Head Start programmes, however, were more widespread and are the ones which concern us here.

While most of the work in the area of the disadvantaged, both in an analysis of the problem and in attempts to deal with it, has been carried out in the United States (a cursory glance at a bibliography of such work is enough to make this clear — *cf*. Bloom, Davis and Hess, 1965; Van Leer Foundation, 1971), over the past few years, there has been a growing interest in problems of the disadvantaged in Europe and a number of studies are now under way in several countries (e.g., Goldschmidt and Sommerkorn, 1970; Roman, 1974; Stukát, 1974a, 1974b). Interest in problems underlying disadvantage is not new in Britain, and there have been several studies relating social class membership and home background to school attainment and educational opportunity (e.g., Burt, 1937; Douglas, 1964; Floud, Halsey and Martin, 1957; Fraser, 1959; Great Britain: Department of Education and Science, 1967; Wiseman, 1964). However, to date, relatively little, by comparison with the United States, has been done on the development and evaluation of intervention procedures to deal with problems of the disadvantaged (*cf*. Nisbet, 1970; G. Williams, 1970; Wiseman, 1968; Wiseman and Goldman, 1970). Studies for which reports are now available are, one carried out by the NFER (H.L. Williams, 1973; Woodhead, 1976), one in Swansea (Schools Council, 1968) and others, which, following the recommendations of the Plowden Report (Great Britain: Department of Education and Science, 1967), have been carried out in a number of Educational

Priority Areas (Barnes, 1975; Halsey, 1972; Midwinter, 1972; Morrison, Watt and Lee, 1974; Payne, 1974; G. Smith, 1975). The scale of these operations has not been very large. Perhaps the problem of disadvantage in Britain is less severe than in the United States. At any rate, research funds on the same scale as in America have not been available to tackle the problem in Britain (*cf.* H.L. Williams, 1973).

The situation in Europe generally is not very different to that in Britain. Only initial signs of activity in the field of disadvantage were perceptible in 1967 when the UNESCO Institute for Education in Hamburg organized a meeting on Deprivation and Disadvantage (Passow, 1970). Activity has increased considerably in the last few years as is witnessed by the publications, symposia and seminars of the Council of Europe (*cf.* Council of Europe, Documentation Centre for Education in Europe, 1971a, 1971b, 1974). European projects, inevitably, have drawn considerably on American experience, since a great deal of work had already been carried out in the United States. We may hope that, in the future, a cross-fertilization of the American and European traditions in education will bring us further along the road in an understanding of the problems of disadvantage and in formulating solutions to deal with those problems. In the meanwhile we have to rely largely on the American experience.

Attempts at evaluation were built into Head Start and other individual programmes right from the start. Despite this fact, unequivocal information about the effectiveness of the intervention is not available. Part of the reason for this is to be found in difficulties inherent in the evaluation of programmes of this kind and part is to be found in the diversity of programmes in terms of their objectives and approaches (McDill, McDill and Sprehe, 1972). Criticism of pre-school intervention programmes reached its highest visibility level in Jensen's (1969) paper 'How much can we boost IQ and scholastic achievement?' Jensen's argument was basic and relatively uncomplicated: the failure of compensatory education to produce lasting effects on children's IQ and attainment was because IQ is largely determined by genetic factors, and so, one cannot hope to alter it by environmental means. Rejoiners to his position inevitably pointed to studies that document the role of experience in the development of intelligence (Elkind, 1969) and also to the finding that while traditional pre-school programmes which emphasized play may be of little value in altering children's cognitive skills, some programmes were showing some success (Hunt, 1969); in other words, though many intervention approaches might have failed, it did not follow that the possibility of successful intervention should be discounted.

Jensen's review of the effectiveness of pre-school programmes was not the only one. Around the same time a large scale empirical investigation of Head Start programmes – the most comprehensive and systematic to date – was carried out by the Westinghouse Learning Corporation and Ohio University (1969). In this study, which had an *ex post facto* or quasi-experimental design (i.e., the control group was not identified until criterion variables were to be measured), data were obtained on the cognitive and affective behaviour of several thousand children who had taken part in summer and full-year Head Start programmes in 104 communities throughout the United States. At the time of the study, children were entering first, second and third grades. Information was also obtained for a sample of control children. The report found little to enthuse about in pre-school compensatory programmes. In the first grade, children who had spent a full year in Head Start (but not those who had only taken part in summer programmes) performed better than controls on the Metropolitan Readiness Test, but by their second year they had lost this advantage. On other measures (e.g., Illinois Test of Psycholinguistic Abilities, Stanford Achievement Tests, Children's Self-Concept Index), Head Start children did not differ appreciably from their school peers who had not attended Head Start.

Detailed criticisms of the study have been put forward (Campbell and Erlebacher, 1970; Smith and Bissell, 1970). These related to inadequacies in sampling, to the narrowness of the scope of the study (focussing on cognitive and affective criteria), to the validity of criterion variables (particularly those relating to cognitive criteria) and to the disadvantages of the *ex post facto* experimental design which involved attempts to match subjects on relevant variables and the use of a covariance random replications model. The debate between the critics of the Report and its authors (Cicirelli, 1970; Cicirelli, Evans and Schiller, 1970; Evans and Schiller, 1970) was, however, to a large extent academic. The finding of the Westinghouse study that most Head Start programmes had relatively little measured impact was basically in agreement with most other evaluations. In most cases where an effect was demonstrated, it was slight and short-lived.

If most early attempts at compensatory education had largely failed (Jensen, 1969; Cronbach, 1969), part of the reason, it seemed, could be that children had not been provided with the most relevant kind of learning experience in the pre-school (Hunt, 1969). Most Head Start programmes operated in the context of traditional nursery school education; no other model was available. Such education set out in a general way 'to stimulate creative expression, provide for the acquisition of information, and offer learning opportunities in such areas as language, communication, motor and social skills' (Swift, 1964, p. 261). In practice, nursery school programmes seemed to place considerable emphasis on social and personality development (*cf.* Sears and Dowley, 1963). Bereiter and Engelmann (1966) pointed out that this kind of approach was geared to the needs of the middle class child, complementing the activities of the homes of such children and, indeed, in some ways resembling the activities of a lower class environment. The middle class home, for example, is rich in verbal experience while the nursery school stresses seeing and doing. The needs of the working class child, however, were very different; what these children needed in the pre-school were activities that complement the activities of the disadvantaged home and are similar to those of the middle class home, i.e., activities that focus on cognitive, language and other school-related skills. Most directors of Head Start programmes, however, reported 'a preference for a supportive unstructured, socialization programme rather than a structured informational' one (Boyd, 1966, p. 38). Gordon and Wilkerson (1966) describe pre-school intervention programmes as attempting to provide

> a warm accepting atmosphere in which a child may achieve his own maximum social and physical development, and an ordered atmosphere in which selected equipment and activities are offered in sufficient variety to meet each child's level of interest and ability (p. 48).

Thus pre-school programmes for disadvantaged were not, on the whole, providing the kind of environment and activities that Bereiter and Engelmann felt were needed.

There were other reasons why the Head Start intervention programmes might not have been as successful as their originators had hoped. The whole effort suffered from a general lack of organization; centres were practically autonomous. Programmes also suffered from lack of preparation, planning and teacher-training. This lack of thought, organization and planning are hardly surprising when one considers the speed at which the operation was mounted. The relevant planning committee was established in November 1964, the programme was announced in January 1965 and was operational on a national basis in the summer of the same year (Smith and Bissell, 1970). That kind of time, given all the enthusiasm in the world, was hardly adequate to deal with one of the most intractable problems in the whole of education.

More recently, a number of Head Start centres have adopted programmes, which compared to the original Head Start efforts, were better formulated, had undergone testing and were based on a more thorough analysis of the needs of disadvantaged children. These programmes participated in the Head Start Planned Variation Study, which began in 1969, and have been classified under three main headings (Bissell, 1973): pre-academic programmes (fostering the development of pre-academic skills, such as number and letter recognition), cognitive discovery programmes (promoting the growth of basic cognitive processes such as categorization, differentiation and abstraction) and discovery programmes (fostering learning as part of the growth of the 'whole child' through free exploration and free play). Procedures in the evaluation of these approaches share many of the shortcomings of earlier evaluations (Datta, 1975). Their findings are basically similar, pointing to greater, but relatively short-term, gains in achievement and cognitive development for participating children than for non-participating children (M.S. Smith, 1975).

Pre-school intervention programmes at the local level suffered less from the kinds of pressures and disadvantages that had been associated with Head Start. They were on a smaller scale, more carefully designed and executed and more attention was given to planning and the choice of activities. Frequently, the programmes were associated with academic institutions, which might suggest that a sounder theoretical basis for the design of the programme and its activities was available. Frequently too, additional staff were available who were specially recruited for the project, which did not have to fit into an already established school programme. Finally, many were longitudinal in nature and, since evaluation procedures were more rigorous, probably more confidence can be placed in their findings. It is of interest that such studies provide the strongest evidence on the effectiveness of pre-school intervention programmes that is available, more positive findings being reported for them than for the component programmes of the large-scale Head Start (Beller, 1973; Gray and Klaus, 1970; Klaus and Gray, 1968; Weikart, 1967, 1968; Weikart, Deloria, Lawser, and Wiegerink, 1970).

An examination of relatively successful programmes reveals certain elements which they have in common. Before looking at these, it is useful to consider two dimensions along which programmes can be differentiated (Stodolsky, 1972). One is structure. In a structured programme, the teacher emphasizes specific goals. Furthermore, the pursuit of those goals is adhered to by allocating specific times for relevant activities, by providing suitable materials and by prescribing children's responses. By comparison with unstructured approaches, the structured one is more teacher-directed and more homogeneous in its activities. Examples of such approaches are the Bereiter and Engelmann (1966) language programme and the programmes of the Perry Pre-school Project in Ypsilanti (Weikart, 1971). Unstructured programmes are sometimes called traditional, child-centred or discovery programmes. The child self-selects his activities rather than being directed towards a particular activity by the teacher. Traditional nursery school programmes are usually low in structure. Though such traditional programmes are often termed child-centred, by comparison with more structured approaches they are child-centred only insofar as the selection of activities is concerned. A structured programme, such as one based on Piagetian principles of development, could be child-centred to the extent that the choice of activities and materials is based on developmental principles and related to individual differences.

The other basis on which pre-school programmes have been differentiated is whether the programme emphasizes intellectual-scholastic goals or socio-emotional ones. This was the distinction which was put forward so cogently by Bereiter and Engelmann. Degree of structure is not a necessary correlate of scholastic bias in a programme. In practice, however, most of the highly structured programmes have been ones that emphasized cognitive and scholastic goals.

While most programmes might seem of little value, Hawkridge and his associates (Hawkridge, Chalupsky and Roberts, 1968; Hawkridge, Tallmadge and Larsen, 1968) decided to identify and examine those that did seem effective. They identified programmes which seemed to show some success, i.e., those in which children showed gains on measures of cognitive ability (IQ, reading or mathematics). Out of 1,000 programmes investigated, about a hundred could, with reasonable confidence, be said to fall into this category. They then attempted to identify the factors which most frequently discriminated successful from unsuccessful programmes. They found that successful programmes were characterized by a statement of scholastic objectives and careful planning to attain them, small groups with individualized attention, the availability of relevant materials, high intensity of treatment and relevant teacher-training. Very similar factors were identified in other studies of the characteristics of successful projects (McDill, McDill, and Sprehe, 1969; Posner, 1968). These characteristics, it will be noted, all fit into the concept of a structured programme geared to intellectual-scholastic objectives.

Further consideration of the more successful Head Start and small-scale studies leads to further generalizations about pre-school intervention. These generalizations are made at the risk of over-simplification and, in our present state of knowledge, are more correctly regarded as guidelines rather than as detailed or definitive statements. The generalizations, which vary in the degree of supporting evidence they receive in the literature, are presented in thirteen statements, drawn from a variety of reviews of empirical studies of the effectiveness of pre-school education (Beller, 1973; Bronfenbrenner, 1974; Di Lorenzo *et al.*, 1969; Karnes, 1969; Kellaghan, 1972; Mayer, 1971; McDill, McDill, and Sprehe, 1972; Smith and Bissell, 1970).

(i)   Pre-school programmes can produce substantial gains in IQ.

(ii) Programmes which have clearly stated cognitive objectives are more successful than ones which have not.

(iii) Programme content may have specific effects on children's performance. While a general measure of performance (such as Stanford-Binet IQ) may not discriminate between programmes, all of which have been well planned and implemented (Karnes, 1973; Di Lorenzo and Salter, 1968; Weikart, 1969, 1972), a number of studies provide evidence of effects which are specific to the content of a programme in addition to a more general programme effect (Bissell, 1973; Halsey, 1972; G. Smith, 1975; Woodhead, 1976).

(iv) A high level of verbal interactive behaviour between adults and children seems important.

(v) Structure is a feature of most successful programmes. However, structure may not in itself be critical (Karnes, 1969; Turner, in press). The failure of structured programmes, such as the Montessori approach, to lead to improvement in the performance of disadvantaged children (Karnes, 1973; Di Lorenzo and Salter, 1968) in the absence of added emphasis on language development (Kohlberg, 1968) has led to the suggestion that extent of meaningful adult—child interaction may be more important than structure (Woodhead, 1976). In general, a balance between drill and the pupil's freedom to initiate activities seems desirable (Soar and Soar, 1972).

(vi) Gains from pre-schooling tend to disappear after intervention is terminated. Not much effect has been found beyond the second grade.

(vii) On an *a priori* basis, length of programme would seem to be a significant factor. However, the relationship between the length of time spent in a programme and the magnitude of the effects of the programme does not seem to be linear. While a full-year programme seems more effective than a short-term (summer) one in producing cognitive gains, evidence is not available that extending the programme beyond three or four terms will continue to produce effects of a similar magnitude to those produced in the first year.

(viii) Meticulous planning and lucidly stated programme objectives are important.

(ix) Individualization of instruction is also important. This usually presupposes a low pupil—adult ratio.

(x) Instructional activities and materials should be closely tied to programme objectives.

(xi) Training of teachers in the methods and content of the programme is necessary.

(xii) The children who benefit most are those from less deprived social and economic backgrounds; children from large one-parent families, in which there is a poor parental and employment record, benefit least.

(xiii) Without the involvement of the home, there is little prospect of intervention being successful (I.J. Gordon, 1975; Karnes, 1973). The provision of family services, health and nutritional care helps, as well as the involvement of the mother in the actual educational development of the child.

As already indicated, these generalizations, given our present state of knowledge, must be regarded as tentative. Some may prefer to regard them as working hypotheses. Most would agree that they are in need of further exploration and confirmation.

Chapter III

The Pre-school Project

The rest of this book is concerned with the description and evaluation of a pre-school project for disadvantaged children in central Dublin. In this chapter, the area in which the pre-school is based is described. This is followed by a brief description of the pre-school, which caters for approximately 180 children, aged three and four years. The curriculum outline used in the project is then briefly described. On the basis of this outline, teachers developed activities and materials which were designed to help children achieve the broad cognitive-scholastic objectives of the curriculum. Finally, in this chapter, the efforts of the pre-school to involve parents are described.

Succeeding chapters describe the procedures used to evaluate the effectiveness of the pre-school project and the results of the evaluation.

The area and its population

The area in which the pre-school is based is predominantly residential with little commercial or industrial activity. Seventy-four per cent of the population live in two or three-room apartments (Carney *et al.*, 1970). Material poverty is an ever-present reality in the lives of a high proportion of families, unemployment seeming to be the greatest single factor in keeping many families at subsistence level. Unemployment figures fluctuate with the general economic situation and time of year; in a survey carried out in the area in the late 1960s, 30 per cent of the adult males were unemployed (Carney *et al.*, 1970). Some of the unemployment may be explained by the fact that many people in the area seem to lack the physical and mental skills which would enable them to hold a steady job. Among the employed, the majority hold semi-skilled or unskilled jobs. A few are self-employed. Only about five per cent are in fully skilled employment. Many mothers are forced to seek part-time work (mainly cleaning work) to supplement the family income.

The kinds of human problems which are present in all areas and at all levels of society exist in an extreme form in the project area. The parents whose children are likely to be at educational risk may have one or more of the following characteristics in addition to unemployment: chronic ill-health, inability to match resources to needs, inadequate accommodation, large families, one or both parents under twenty at marriage, disharmony amounting at times to ill-treatment and desertion, addiction to alcohol or gambling, frequent and prolonged absences from home, inadequate knowledge of the developmental needs of their children and a lack of understanding of the purpose of school.

Yet these parents, although beset by personal and social problems of this magnitude, make great sacrifices to provide for the physical and recreational needs of their children. They provide clothes, toys and pocket money in a measure which would often appear to be beyond their means. They show signs of acute distress when their children are ill. It may be pertinent to observe that they show as much concern for their children as parents in any other social group. However, many seem to be ill-equipped to cater for the cognitive needs of their children. The question of homework may serve as an example. The setting of homework, which usually involves the application at home of some principle explained in school, is common practice in most schools in Ireland. It is well known that parents who try to make the best use of the available educational opportunites expect teachers to assign homework and they are quite happy to supervise it. Parents of disadvantaged children, however, not only do not expect homework to be given but are usually unable to supervise it or even to provide the kinds of physical conditions in which it could be done. This attitude to homework is part of a more general attitude towards school-related activities. A connection between success in school and success in life is often spoken about, but it has seldom been clearly demonstrated to the parents of disadvantaged children. Their own school experience may have been harsh and unsatisfactory. In the Carney *et al.* (1970) survey, 30 per cent of parents in the area had left school by fifth standard in the primary school, a further 38 per cent left in sixth standard, while the education of a further 21 per cent terminated in seventh standard. Only three per cent had passed the primary certificate examination. Obviously for these parents the school was not a vehicle of social mobility or the path to success in later life. It is difficult to expect such parents to provide the kind of psychological support which would enable their children to develop positive attitudes about the value of school. It is also true that those educational experiences, which are independent of school, such as those associated with travelling, holidays, visits to museums and art galleries, are unlikely to be made available by the parents of disadvantaged children.

About the time the project was being planned, a team of

psychologists carried out a study of the educational performance of children between the ages of nine and thirteen in the group of national schools serving the area. One striking result of the survey was that the children were found to have a mean IQ of 83.3 (SD: 13.5) on an individual test of intelligence (McGee, 1970). Attainment in the basic subjects was correspondingly poor. The mean English Quotient on the Marino Word Recognition Test was 73.0 (SD: 17.9), while the mean Arithmetic Quotient on the Vernon Graded Arithmetic Test was 75.4 (SD: 13.1) (Chamberlain, 1970). The findings of this survey point clearly to the existence of a group of children who could, by any criterion, be regarded as in educational need. They confirmed what educationists had long felt about educational standards in the area and demonstrated clearly that traditional educational arrangements were failing, here as elsewhere, to cater for the special needs of disadvantaged children.

The pre-school

The pre-school building has six teaching areas and a central general purpose area. It can accommodate 90 children at any one time. By working morning and afternoon sessions with separate groups of children, it is possible to double the number of children served. Each of six classroom teachers teaches two sessions a day. Attendance, therefore, is on a half-day basis; each teacher takes a group of fifteen children from 9.30 to 12.00 and another group from 1.00 until 3.30. Each teacher is assisted by a classroom aide. Three months before commencing to teach in the pre-school, teachers took part in a pre-service training course in which literature on the disadvantaged was studied and a draft curriculum was drawn up.

Three social workers were appointed to work with families on a case-work basis and to try to make parents more aware of the aims and functions of the school. A nursery nurse to care for the physical needs of the children was also appointed. Finally, a project director had general responsibility for the management of the project.

A feature of the pre-school, which is not common in Irish schools, was the provision of a cooked meal for the children in the middle of the day. Apart from their nutritional value, the meals provide many opportunities for language and social training in the classroom where they are served.

After two years in the pre-school, it was planned that the children should proceed to an adjacent junior school. Many of them did, though quite a large number also went to other schools because their families had moved from the area or because their parents chose to send them elsewhere. A new building was provided for the junior school and adaptations to the normal school curriculum were made to suit the needs of this particular group of children. These adaptations were, on the whole, left to the discretion of individual teachers in consultation with the director of the project. The main thrust of the experimental programme was thus in the pre-school, and it was at this level that major efforts in curriculum development were made. The description of the curriculum that follows refers only to the pre-school level.

The curriculum

A major feature of the project was seen to be the development of a curriculum suitable for three- and four-year-old children living in a disadvantaged area. Several nursery schools operate throughout Ireland, but here as in other countries, the schools mainly serve middle class children. This has obvious implications for the school curriculum; school activities tend to complement the activities of the middle class home and to help make up for deficiencies in the home by providing such things as social experience with other children and freedom to carry on activities often restricted in the middle class home. It seemed very doubtful that a programme made up only of undirected free play activities of the type common in nursery schools would provide the most advantageous experiences for children from a disadvantaged neighbourhood (Bereiter and Engelmann, 1966). If our children are similar to children living in disadvantaged areas elsewhere, then it is likely that they need assistance in the development of language, perceptual and general cognitive skills. Hence, it was felt that a curriculum should include very definite attempts to aid the development of these skills and provide activities that would complement those of the poorer home. To do this, a certain amount of structuring in the choice of materials, activities and content was felt to be desirable.

The curriculum then was planned primarily with cognitive-scholastic objectives in mind. In general terms, the objective of the curriculum was to develop skills that would facilitate adaptation to the work of the primary school. More specifically, this involves the development of skills of perceptual discrimination, the extension of the child's knowledge of the world, particularly of his immediate environment, the development of skills in the organization of knowledge (e.g., classificatory skills) and the development of language skills (in particular, vocabulary).

While the main emphasis was on cognitive development in the pre-school programme, in practice, of course, such development cannot be divorced from other aspects of behaviour, especially from personality and social development. In all the teacher's interactions with the child, even though the main purpose of the interaction may be the development of cognitive behaviour, personality and social factors come into play. Thus, opportunities in which the teacher may influence the personal and social functioning of the child inevitably present themselves. Besides, personality factors may play a large part in adapting to school and in the child's learning. Thus, the curriculum also had the general objective of assisting the general social and personality development of the child.

A second major feature of the curriculum was that it involved some element of structuring. This means, that insofar as it was possible, teachers specified objectives (at least in general terms) and then planned activities that were designed to work towards the attainment of those objectives. Materials that might be required for the activities were made available to the children and specific times were allocated for the activities. Not everything the child did, of course, was prescribed in this way. He also had opportunities during the day to select and pursue his own activities. However, every effort was made to see that for part of the day the child — either on his own initiative or that of the teacher — was exposed to sequences that had been designed to contribute towards the attainment of the goals of the programme.

Although an outline curriculum was provided for the teachers, it was not intended that the minute-to-minute actions of the teachers should be prescribed. The curriculum was no more than its title indicated — an outline, a frame-of-reference within which teachers could work. It was designed to help to focus the teacher's mind on aspects of development that seem important and relevant to future school work. It also encouraged teachers to plan their work carefully, with specific objectives and sequences designed toward the attainment of these objectives in mind. But there never was any doubt that each teacher would implement the curriculum in her own way, nor was it intended that anything else should be attempted. The curriculum did not try to lay down detailed instructions for action in the classroom and there can be little doubt that there were considerable differences in practice between the approaches of the different teachers in the project. Nevertheless, insofar as they accepted the draft curriculum, they all shared common objectives and a common frame-of-reference as they devised their day-to-day activities.

Only a brief summary of the rationale of the curriculum will be considered here. The teachers, of course, had to devise activities that exemplified the general principles of the curriculum. Information on these activities is not included here. It is hoped, however, that sufficient information is presented to allow the reader to obtain a general idea of the approach in the pre-school.

The development of the curriculum was strongly influenced by Piagetian principles of development. Piaget has described strategies used by the child to bring order, meaning and control to his environment, and his theory is the only comprehensive one in existence that analyses a four-year-old's knowledge in terms of his past and his future (Kamii, 1971). It allows for many of the activities of the traditional pre-school, but adds depth and a developmental perspective to them. Furthermore, it emphasizes abilities and skills related to performance at school. Kamii (1971) has indicated how later school work may depend on the development of abilities outlined by Piaget. For example, mechanical reading requires a well-structured space to discriminate letters (p vs q) and to conserve directions (left to right). The grouping of letters into words requires a classificatory scheme. For reading comprehension, a child must have 'the mobility of thought to coordinate the relationships among objects in space, time and logic.' Kamii gives as an example the passage 'John went to the circus with his sister and father; there he saw elephants and clowns', and goes on to point out that the sentence involves space (home and circus are spatial concepts), time (they saw the elephants during the time spent at the circus), classification (part of the family, animals, clowns, i.e., some people), seriation (sister of, brother of, father of), number (three people, some elephants), social knowledge (circus, clowns, elephants at a circus) and physical knowledge (knowledge of the elephants' weight and natural habitat is involved in appreciating the passage). The relevance of Piaget's concepts to arithmetic is also pointed out by Kamii. The problem 'Mary went to the shop with 15 pence and bought 5 pence worth of sweets; how much did she have left?' involves number, class inclusion (15—5), seriation (equal to), temporal sequence (Mary left the house, bought sweets . . .) and social knowledge (shop, money, buy). These examples indicate that while a curriculum based on Piagetian principles might primarily tend to foster the development of general intellectual and cognitive skills, the skills also seem highly relevant to the work of the classroom.

The curriculum outline will be considered under three broad headings: firstly, general cognitive development, secondly, language development and thirdly, personality and social development. While the cognitive programme is presented separately from the other two, all three in practice will be interwoven. In the recommended cognitive activities for example, there is ample opportunity for the use of language. Besides, language must play a large part in the acquisition of concepts and ideas. 'Language', Piaget (1950, p. 159) has noted, 'conveys to the individual an already prepared system of ideas, classifications, relations — in short, an inexhaustible stock of concepts which are reconstructed in each individual after the age-old pattern which previously moulded earlier generations.'

Several curricula for pre-school children based on Piaget's work have been drawn up in recent years. In developing the curriculum for the present study we have drawn on the work of Kamii (1970), Kamii and

Radin (1970), Sonquist, Kamii and Derman (1970) and Weikart, Rogers, Adcock and McClelland (1971).

Cognitive development

The programme on cognitive development reflects a particular point of view on the nature of cognitive behaviour and intelligence, and their development. Basically, intelligence is seen as a repertoire of ways of structuring the environment which is built up through the child's interactions with the world around him. We are subject to an enormous array and diversity of stimuli at all times. The child's developmental task is to bring order to this variety of stimuli. There is not just one order; reality can be represented in many ways. It is the function of education to develop strategies in the child for ordering his world.

There is the further question of developing selectivity to stimuli and models. The perception of the *relevance* of bits of information is always important in problem-solving. It is not easy to say how one develops the ability to select the bits of information relevant to the solution of a problem, but it is possible to identify some skills which the ability seems to pre-suppose. Apart from the fact that one must have categories to which to refer new information, one must also have facility in shifting from one frame of reference to another. Thus the child should be given opportunities to develop flexibility in thinking.

An important aspect of cognitive development is the interaction of the child with his environment. He has to learn at first hand about the physical world — the properties of objects, how things interact, what the results of actions on physical objects are. The child has to learn not only that this object stretches when pulled, but has to learn the characteristic 'stretching' itself. The curriculum should provide plenty of opportunity for the child to interact with his environment and explore objects he comes in contact with. Thus, there should be opportunities for handling objects and observing, stretching, breaking, bouncing, squeezing, bending, pouring (liquid, sand), floating.

Very often the homes of disadvantaged children are lacking in manipulable toys and objects. More is probably involved than just an absence of objects from which one could derive knowledge of the physical world, however. Parents of disadvantaged children probably differ from parents of middle class children in their attitudes towards, and guidance of, the young child's exploration of his environment, and particularly in their readiness to discuss things. Hence the pre-school curriculum should attempt to inculcate attitudes of inquiry, exploration and explanation. While one should work towards the explanation of events, at this stage of development, the emphasis in practice should be on prediction ('If I let this fall . . . ,') rather than on explanation (Kamii and Radin, 1970).

On the basis of his interactions with the environment, the child has to learn to order the infinite number of stimuli he encounters. In Bruner's words, to operate effectively in an environment, an organism must develop a model of the environment, and this for at least two reasons:

> In the first place, it is a way of conserving information in the form of concepts or universals, the means whereby — to use Aristotelian language — we separate essences from accidents, or in modern terms, signal from noise. If you will, the recurrent regularities and the higher probability relationships between and among events are conserved in this model. Given such models . . . it becomes possible, secondly, for an organism to extrapolate and interpolate on the basis of partial information, to perform the kind of inference that may be called, 'going beyond the information given' (Bruner, 1961, p. 200).

Piaget has considered certain strategies which the child uses in organizing his environment. These involve classification (which of course presupposes the ability to discriminate), seriation, one-to-one correspondence, conservation, the structuring of space and the structuring of time. Activities towards furthering the development of such strategies were a feature of the work of the pre-school.

Finally, the child has to learn to move away from the constraints of the immediate environment in his thinking. In other words, his modes of thought have to become more abstract. The ability to attend effectively to a variety of stimuli involves the development of selective attention, of increasing periods of concentration, and of the ability to shift attention and bases of classification as needed.

Language development

The programme is based on the assumption that language, particularly vocabulary, plays a major role in cognitive development and that language is intimately related to the child's development of more flexible and abstract modes of thought. While some of the goals in the programme are directed towards improving inter-individual communications (e.g., towards having the child form good sentences), the main emphasis is on assisting the general cognitive development of the child and in particular in the use of language for 'inter-individual communication' (i.e., thinking).

While many pre-school curricula include a special language programme, language of course will never be confined to a single period. Extensive language usage usually does, and always should, run right through the entire schoolday. Children may differ in their understanding of when and how to use speech. The curriculum should provide opportunities for the child to increase the number of functions for which he uses speech. He should learn more and more to use verbal means to express ideas and feelings (*ask* for what he wants, *protest* rather than hurt someone, ask *questions*, express feelings etc.). The first general principle then relating to language is to encourage its use in a variety of contexts. The sheer extent of verbal interaction between adult and child seems very important.

A second general principle is that verbal communication is probably more effective when supported by other kinds of information. It is well to relate conversations to things the child is currently interested in or is actually doing. Thirdly, one should use a variety of contexts: many different situations, different stories. One should also use a variety of linguistic forms, i.e., there should be variety in vocabulary and in grammatical patterns.

Much actual language usage will occur spontaneously, depending on the situation in which teacher and child meet. The teacher can however, even apart from formal language programmes, use conversations with children to work towards certain objectives. First of all, the child's perception and understanding of 'reality' can be furthered through the use of language. Language can be used to make statements about reality. 'This is a box.' 'This is a boy.' 'This is a ball.' Here we are really concerned with vocabulary development. Vocabulary, of course, is infinite and some selection has to be made. That is, the teacher must consider what words or kinds of words she wants the children to learn. Various criteria may be used in the selection of words. Words may relate to the immediate environment, the child's home, or they may be the kind of words used in the early years of school. Again, one may include words of varying degrees of abstractness. Or one may select words from lists of most commonly used words. The kinds of stories one chooses are also related to what kind of vocabulary one feels the children should learn. In the development of curricular practices, teachers met and exchanged information about vocabulary development, choosing stories, analyzing the vocabulary involved and children's reactions.

Secondly, the qualities or attributes of objects in the environment can be described in language. (The book is red; the block is blue; the grass is green). Language presumably helps in developing the child's discriminations and, in turn, his ability to classify objects. Similarities and differences between objects are to be noted. While in classificatory behaviour one does not necessarily verbalize the criterial attribute, at times this may be useful (e.g., 'Pick out all the red ones' rather than 'Pick out all the ones like this'). Used in this way, language can play a role in the development of the logical behaviour of classification.

Thirdly, language can be a powerful means of relating and

sequencing events. The spatial relationships of events may be expressed in language ('This is *beside* that'). Statements about spatial relationships may concern objects that are visually present (as in the classroom). But they may also refer to objects that are absent ('Tell me the way you go home', 'What is beside the church?' etc.). Likewise, and this can be quite difficult, events in time can be related in language (something happened before this; then something else happened; after that . . .). Children should be provided with opportunities to describe what happened last evening or during the morning at school or on a trip.

An important form of sequencing is planning. A child may be asked to say what he is going to do during the next period; how he would achieve a certain objective (e.g., if he wanted to paint, what would he have to do). The length of time over which children state their plans can be gradually increased. Stories may also be used to develop sequencing ability; a child can be asked to recall a story, while the teacher pays particular attention to the sequence of events: 'What happened next?' 'Did anything happen before that?'

Pictures and cartoons can also be used for sequencing: e.g., putting a series of pictures together to make a story. But this is primarily a non-verbal approach.

Personality and social development

Personality and social development is an extremely complex area and covers such diverse topics as social development, motivation, the development of self-concept and the development of independence. Here we will treat only the general social development of the child, considering personality development as a form of role-learning. Even a young child plays many roles. He takes one role when dealing with his parents and another when dealing with other children; this role will vary with the age of the other children, and with whether or not they are members of his family. Yet again, the child's behaviour will follow a different pattern when he is dealing with the teacher and with other adults. As the child grows older, the number of roles he plays increases and the facility with which he plays them also improves (*cf.* Flavell *et al.*, 1968).

The behaviour of young children has frequently been described as egocentric or self-centred. Many indications of this have been noted, such as solitary and on-looking 'group' behaviour. During the pre-school years, there is a decrease in solitary play and in on-looking and an increase in associative and cooperating activity. Thus social interaction and participation increases through the pre-school years.

The term egocentricity has been applied not only to social behaviour, but to logical behaviour as well. Not only is the child poorly skilled in his social behaviour, he is also unable to take the perspective of another person in his thinking. For Piaget, children's thinking up to the age of seven is largely egocentric. He notes that the child rarely questions whether or not his ideas are understood by others, he doesn't attempt to see the other person's point of view and his language and thought are generally self-centred (Piaget, 1959).

Elsewhere Piaget (1950) has stressed the importance of social collaboration for the child's intellectual development. For Piaget, the main trend in the development of intelligence is towards a decentralization of the thought processes, a freeing of the individual's perceptions and thoughts from egocentricity. This is impossible without the assistance of the social group. ' . . . It is precisely by a constant interchange of thought with others that we are able to decentralize ourselves in this way, to coordinate internally relations deriving from different viewpoints' (Piaget, 1950, p. 164). Logical thought then is necessarily social; an individual arrives at logic as the result of cooperation and the free interchange of ideas with other people.

Social development can be considered as having three components. Firstly, there is social knowledge: the individual must learn what is expected of him in various roles. This involves learning not only what is appropriate to the roles he himself will play, but also something of the other roles he will encounter in life. He will have to be able to identify and discriminate in new situations; in many cases, generalizations from similar situations encountered in the past will be required. Secondly, the child has to learn social skills, i.e., he must learn the skills necessary to meet the demands of different roles. This will involve trying new responses and evaluating one's performance. And thirdly, social development involves motivation: one may have the knowledge and skills, and yet not apply them in a given situation. One must be motivated to act in what is considered an appropriate manner. One also has to appreciate the desirability of behaving differently in different social situations.

Play provides an obvious opportunity for the child to interact with other children and with an adult and it may help children in developing basic roles related to other children and adults. In the fantasy that often is a part of play, a child gets opportunities to learn of roles other than those with which he might have come into direct contact. Play may be dramatic without involving interactions with others. To be socio-dramatic however, interactions with others must be involved; these may be non-verbal as well as verbal. According to Sara Smilansky (1968), socio-dramatic play involves interaction with at least one other person, make-believe roles taken by the child, roles expressed in imitative action and verbalization, actions and verbalizations as substitutes for real objects and situations, sustained verbal interaction and play lasting at least ten minutes. Some children may not at certain times cooperate in play activities. A child's willingness to play can depend on many factors, among them, his attitude towards his proposed companions and his interest in the topic of play. Teachers may have to experiment with many different situations to involve some children.

Parents
    While the pre-school centre was the focal point of the project, the active involvement of parents was seen as being necessary for the success of the project. Before the project began, feelings of indifference and hostility towards school were prevalent among parents. Unless such negative attitudes could be changed, any benefit the children might derive from their experience in the pre-school centre would be likely to be shortlived. So an important objective of the project was to involve parents, and particularly the mothers, as closely as possible in the work of the school. The teachers were asked to keep this aspect of their work clearly in mind. The first group of teachers visited the home of every child in their class before the child entered the school. They spoke to the mother and child at home. They found this visit helped them to have a clearer picture of the child and it provided an opportunity to meet the mother and other members of the family. It has since become established practice that someone from the school visits the child at home prior to admission to school. Parents are encouraged to bring their children to school, to spend some time in the classroom and to participate in the classroom activities. Every effort is made to build up a relationship with parents based on understanding and mutual respect and to convince the parents that they have an important contribution to make to their children's scholastic progress.
    Parent—teacher meetings were held in the school in the evenings. A letter was sent to each home in advance of the meeting outlining its purpose and asking for the attendance of both parents. The teacher endeavoured to make personal contact with the mother of each child a day or two before the meeting to remind her of the day and time and to express the hope that the child's father would attend. The average attendance of parents at meetings was 10 fathers and 50 mothers. A surprising number of parents were prevented from attending by circumstances outside their control. A special effort was made to interest parents who seemed reluctant to come to meetings and only a tiny minority failed to attend at least one. There was also a substantial minority who attended every meeting. The entire staff of the pre-school attended the general meetings. In the case of meetings for particular groups of children, only the teachers and / or social workers immediately involved were in attendance.

The meetings were conducted in a friendly and informal atmosphere but they had a serious purpose. Every effort was made to convince the parents of their own importance in the educational progress of their children. It was pointed out repeatedly that the school on its own could do comparatively little without the active support and cooperation of the home. The educational programme of the school was explained in detail. The relationship between the classroom activities and things like reading and arithmetic was stressed. In general, the parents did not question the approach though this need not necessarily imply that they understood it fully.

It is often said that fathers take little interest in their children's school progress. The experience of the project does not support this. It is true that they did not attend meetings to any great extent but they gave many indications of their willingness to take an active part in the project. One example was the action they took to protect the school against vandalism. About 40 of them volunteered for this work. They agreed to patrol the school building from 8 p.m. until midnight. Two fathers were assigned to the work each night and they were expected to be present one night a month. Moreover, comments made by the mothers to the teachers suggested that many of the fathers were taking a keen interest in what the children were doing in school.

The general atmosphere of the school continues to be one of friendliness and full cooperation with parents who do not convey any sense of inadequacy or inferiority in their relationship with the teachers. This is a hopeful development though hardly a surprising one in view of the fact that a survey carried out in Dublin some years ago revealed that working class parents were almost unanimous in their desire for closer contacts with the schools (Kelly, 1970). When schools take the initiative in attempting to increase parents' involvement in the education of their children, most parents are not likely to reject the opportunities offered.

Chapter IV

The Evaluation of the Project

It was planned that all children in the study should follow the same cognitively-oriented, structured curriculum (an outline of which was presented in Chapter III) for a period of two years in the pre-school. Thus, there was no planned differentiation of treatment, although it is reasonable to assume that teachers differed in the ways they implemented the curriculum. The overall effectiveness of the pre-school programme was assessed by comparing aspects of the scholastic performance of the children who had participated in the programme with the performance of a control group who had not. Thus, in terms of the research approaches outlined by Averch *et al*. (1972), ours was an 'evaluation' approach, i.e., an attempt to assess the overall effectiveness of a broad educational intervention. The basic question in the present case was whether or not intervention of the type carried out in the pre-school contributed towards raising the scholastic performance of the participants.

Ideally, an evaluation should tell one firstly, if the programme objectives have been achieved and secondly, if the programme services accounted for the achievement of the objectives (Stufflebeam *et al*. 1971). The objective of the pre-school programme was to raise the level of scholastic performance of the participants. Level of scholastic performance was operationalized in terms of performance on standardized tests of intelligence as well as performance on standardized tests of attainment in the basic school subjects (English, Irish and mathematics*). Like the present study, most pre-school programmes for disadvantaged children have focussed on the cognitive effects of

---

* Although the mathematical attainment of the control groups was assessed, by the time it came to test the experimental group, decimalization had taken place and it was not possible to use the same tests. Direct comparisons in mathematical attainment were thus not possible.

programmes; indeed most evaluations have used an IQ or achievement measure as the criterion (Bronfenbrenner, 1974; McDill, McDill and Sprehe, 1969). However, non-cognitive outcomes are also regarded as being important (McDill, McDill and Sprehe, 1972). The fact that measurement techniques in the non-cognitive area are relatively poorly developed probably accounts for the fact that they have been used relatively infrequently. While the raising of the level of the scholastic performance of participants was the main objective of our pre-school programme, it was also assumed that changes would occur in other personal characteristics of the children. Thus, a series of personality measures was included in the evaluation.

The selection of a measure of general intellectual development (an intelligence test) as an outcome measure received support from recent comments by Cooley (1974) who outlined criteria which he feels ought to be considered in selecting such measures. Firstly, he notes, the outcome measures should have predictive validity, i.e., they should be useful in predicting success as an adult. Secondly, what they measure should be treatable, i.e., there should be some theoretical or empirical basis for expecting that the outcome measures can be affected by the educational practices being assessed. And thirdly, outcome measures should be parsimonious, i.e., redundancies among them should be reduced to a minimum. According to Cooley, the outcome measure which best satisfies these three criteria is general intellectual development. Cooley's conclusions are obviously open to question. For example, whether intelligence test performance is a good predictor of success in adult life is doubtful. At the same time, considerable stability in intelligence test scores from pre-school years to adolescence has been reported (Bloom, 1964), while early performance on such tests is also reasonably closely related to eventual number of years of school completed (Jencks *et al.*, 1972). The question of treatability is also questionable. However, many pre-school programmes have been based on the assumption that certain practices lead to changes in the intellectual functioning of children as measured by intelligence tests and there is some evidence that such changes can be effected, at least on a temporary basis. On balance, at the time the instruments were selected for the present investigation, there was no obvious and compelling reason for not including an intelligence test as one of our measures of programme outcome.

If our measures of outcome can be regarded as adequate and if at the end of the programme, we find that the participants have, in fact, 'improved' their performance on these measures, then we can say that the programme objectives have been achieved to a greater or lesser extent, depending on the degree of 'improvement'. The second question asks if the improvement can be attributed to the programme services.

We are in a stronger position to answer this question in the positive if we have information on the performance of a control group with which to make comparisons. In the present case, the overall effectiveness of the programme was assessed by comparing the performance of the experimental group who had participated in the programme with that of a control group on a number of tests of cognitive development and attainment. The children were all eight years of age when this comparison was made. If the two groups can be regarded as being alike in all ways, except that one had participated in the pre-school programme, then any differences found between the groups should be attributable to the pre-school programme. Thus, our procedure should answer the second question concerning the cause of the improved achievement.

While our evaluation procedure answers Stufflebeam *et al.*'s (1971) two basic questions concerning an evaluation, it should be noted that it does not permit us to say precisely which features of the programme might be critical in the attainment of the objectives (Averch *et al.*, 1972). In our programme, a number of educational inputs and processes were changed at the same time: children began school earlier than usual, a special curriculum was provided, meals were available and home—school links were fostered. Whether any one of these in isolation or a number of them in combination would have produced similar effects, we cannot say.

One aspect of our evaluation, then, involved the comparison of the performance of the experimental group with that of a control group from a similar background. Data were also collected on the performance of a sample of children from non-disadvantaged backgrounds, thus permitting a comparison of the performance of the two groups from a disadvantaged background with that of children in other areas. Frequently normative data are used for this comparison; however, normative data for an Irish population were not available for most of the tests used in our study.

Information was obtained on the homes of experimental and control groups, relating to status variables (e.g., father's occupation, size of family) and process variables (e.g., parental aspirations, family activities) in the home. The incorporation of this information into analyses provided some indication of relationships between home variables and the personal development of the children.

Evaluation was not confined to a comparison of the performance of experimental and control groups. Other evaluative evidence was collected during the life of the programme. Thus, the cognitive development of the experimental group was monitored during the pre-school years and for the three years following. The main instrument used in this exercise was the Stanford—Binet Intelligence Scale.

Additional information was collected relating to the development of the children's general knowledge and to the development of their reading skills.

Information was also obtained on the reactions of parents to the project. This information was felt to be important, as in the absence of parental acceptance of the pre-school, the project could hardly hope to accomplish much. Besides, the creation of more positive attitudes among parents to themselves as educators as well as towards the school could be seen as an important objective of any pre-school programme for children in a disadvantaged area.

Finally, a number of analyses involving the performance of children within the experimental group were carried out. These were related to such variables as sex, school class membership and length of stay in programme.

Subjects of the investigation
1. *Experimental group*
All children living in a clearly defined geographical area in the centre of Dublin and born between July 1, 1965 and August 31, 1966 were eligible for attendance at the pre-school which commenced operation in September 1969. The project made no attempt to identify and select individual children who were likely to experience learning difficulties beyond the fact that admission to the school was limited to children living in a poor economic area with a high rate of educational failure. In effect, the area, rather than individual members of the population, was judged disadvantaged. This approach was taken for two reasons. First of all, no adequate personal criteria have been established for the identification of disadvantaged children in Ireland. And secondly, even if such criteria had been established and could have been applied, it was not considered desirable that such children should be segregated and treated in a separate school (*cf.* Coleman *et al.*, 1966). Even in an area in which the economic level is poor, one would expect considerable heterogeneity in the characteristics of children and in the attitudes and aspirations of parents. It was decided to retain any heterogeneity that existed in the area in planning special educational provision.

The names of all children born within the relevant dates in the area were ascertained by reference to public records of births. Altogether, 251 names were recorded. Eight part-time social workers were employed to visit the addresses listed for the children at the time of their birth to ascertain if they were still living in the area. If found to be still in the area, the proposed pre-school project was explained to their parents who were also invited to apply for a place for their children in the pre-school. Of the 251 children born in the area in 1965—66, only 109 were still living there in April 1969. A further 22 children, born outside the area between the relevant dates but now living in it were also identified. This gave a total of 131 eligible children and of these, the parents of 121 applied for a place in the pre-school. By November 1969, a total of 96 children (48 boys and 48 girls) had actually taken their places in the school; the families of over 30 of the children had left the area between the time of acceptance and the opening of the pre-school. The children were randomly assigned to one of six classes; three of the classes attended in the morning and three in the afternoon.

On entry, all children participated in a testing programme and information was also obtained on the home environments of the children. There was a certain amount of movement of pupils during the first term of the operation of the pre-school; some children would come for a period and then leave and other children would take their places. It was possible to obtain complete test information for only 90 of the original intake. It is this group of 90 who form the experimental group that is the focus of the present study. Further testing of the children was carried out annually as the group proceeded through the pre-school and the junior school which is adjacent to the pre-school. Not all of the original group were available for testing during the life of the project; some had left the area, a number had left the country. Final testing was carried out when the children were eight years of age. For this testing, every effort was made to trace and contact all the members of the original group; all but five were tested.

There was a continual loss of children during the life of the project. Table 4.1 gives the location of the original experimental group of 90 children over the five years of the project. The most usual reason for leaving the pre-school was the movement of the child's family from the area. The rate of migration slowed down during the project but at the end of the pre-school period, 17 of the original 90 children had moved out of the area and were lost to the project schools. Some parents who continued to live in the area decided to send their children to other schools in the neighbourhood, resulting in the loss of a further 25 children from the experimental group. All except five, however, remained in the Dublin area and their progress in their new school was recorded for the final evaluation of the project.

2. Control group — disadvantaged

All children aged between 8 years 2 months and 9 years 4 months in October 1969 and living in the same geographical area from which participants in the pre-school were recruited formed the population from which a control group was selected. It was ascertained that children in the area attended either a local school or one of a number of schools immediately outside the area which will be referred to as 'neighbouring' schools. Of 180 children in the required age group in the

Table 4.1: Location of original pre-school sample, 1969–1974

Time	Attending Pre-school	Attending junior school	Left area	Attending other school in area	Attending senior school	Unknown
Aug–Dec 1969	90					
Jan–July 1970	88		2			
Aug–Dec 1970	74		8	7		1
Jan–July 1971	73		8	7		2
Aug–Dec 1971		66	12	10		2
Jan–July 1972		62	14	12		2
Aug–Dec 1972		54	19	15		2
Jan–July 1973		50	22	16		2
Aug–Dec 1973		48	24	16		2
Jan–July 1974		44	24	20		2
Aug 1974–		1	29	34	24	2

area, 79 attended the local school and 101 attended one of seven neighbouring schools. A sample of 60 of these (30 boys and 30 girls) was selected for the study. The proportion of children from each school chosen for the sample reflected the proportion of the target population attending the school. Twenty-seven children were selected from the local school and 33 from the neighbouring schools. The mean age of the children in the sample was 8 years 9 months (SD: 5.4 months).

In October and November 1969, these children took part in a testing programme that collected information on their intelligence, language, perceptual development, cognitive style, scholastic attainment and personality. Information was also obtained on their home environments.

3. *Control group – non-disadvantaged*

A further group of children, a so-called 'normal' or non-disadvantaged group was selected from children attending schools in the greater Dublin area. The procedure followed in the selection of this group was that recommended by Burt (1921). This method attempts to identify children of median ability or attainment on the assumption that the scores of such children should approximate the mean of a larger sample of children randomly chosen. For the present study, schools' inspectors were asked to rate schools in their areas in Dublin city and county according to the level of attainment of the pupils. Fifteen median or 'average' schools were thus selected. It was assumed that eight-year-old children of average ability should be found in classes in which the majority of pupils were eight years of age. Where classes were streamed, pupils were selected from the middle stream or from two streams combined. In October 1969, teachers were asked to rank pupils aged between 8 years 2 months and 9 years 4 months for attainment in the selected classes. From those ranked in intermediate positions, 60 pupils (30 boys and 30 girls) were selected randomly. The average number of children selected from each school was 4.13. The mean age of the group was 8 years 7 months (SD: 2.37 months).

These children took the same tests as the disadvantaged control group in October and November 1969; information was also obtained on their home environments.

Variables investigated

A wide range of variables, covering cognitive, scholastic and personality development as well as the home backgrounds of children was used. A listing of the variables follows. The listing and the group for which information on each variable was obtained is provided in summary form in Table 4.2.

Table 4.2: Summary of variables used in evaluation

	Experimental Group					Experimental, Control Disadvantaged, Control Non-Disadvantaged
	Age 3 Stanford–Binet	Age 4 Stanford–Binet	Age 5 Stanford–Binet	Age 6 Stanford–Binet	Age 7 Stanford–Binet	Age 8 Stanford–Binet Cattell Culture Fair
Cognitive						
Perceptual	Visual-Motor Integration Visual Discrim. Auditory Discrim.					Visual-Motor Integration
Language	EPVT ITPA (Gramm. Closure)					EPVT
Cognitive Style						Matching Familiar Figs.
Attainment	Preschool Inventory		Preschool Inventory	Reading Readiness		English Reading Attainment Irish Reading Attainment
Personality	Personality ratings					Personality ratings
Home	Home environment processes					Home environment processes Social class Size of family Ordinal position in family Parents' reactions to pre-school programme*

* Parents of sample of experimental group only.

Cognitive ability

(i) The Stanford—Binet Intelligence Scale (Form L—M) is regarded as a measure of 'general intelligence' (Terman and Merrill, 1961), and has been used in many studies of disadvantaged children. It was administered to the experimental group at ages 3, 4, 5, 6, 7 and 8 and to the two control groups at age eight. (ii) The Cattell Culture Fair Test, Scale 1, is a test of general mental ability, made up of a series of perceptual tasks; a ratio IQ based on chronological and mental ages was calculated (Cattell, 1950). It was administered to experimental and both control groups at age eight.

Visual perceptual ability

Visual perceptual ability has been found to be related to school attainment, particularly reading (*cf.* M.D. Vernon, 1957; Katz and Deutsch, 1967). Two tests of visual perceptual ability were used: (i) The Developmental Test of Visual Motor Integration which is a series of 24 geometric forms to be copied with pencil and paper. The test is designed to examine visual perception and motor coordination. It also involves the coordination of perceptual and motor abilities (*cf.* Beery, 1967). (ii) The Visual Discrimination Inventory is one of a battery of tests developed by Dr Carolyn Stern at the University of California at Los Angeles (Stern, 1967b, 1968). The test assesses the child's ability to discriminate visual stimuli (representational and geometrical) by having the child select from three stimuli the one which matches a standard stimulus. The tasks cover four perceptual areas: form constancy, figure-ground, closure and position-in-space. The Visual-Motor Integration Test was administered to the experimental group at age three and to experimental and both control groups at age eight. The Visual Discrimination Test was administered only to the experimental group at age three.

Auditory perceptual ability

As in the case of visual perceptual ability, auditory perceptual ability is often regarded as an important factor in learning to read. The test included in the present study was The Children's Auditory Discrimination Inventory (Stern, 1967a, 1968). In this test the child is required to discriminate between sounds by pointing to a picture to which a sound label has already been attached. The test was administered to the experimental group at age three.

Language

Two measures of language development were used; both have been used frequently in studies of the disadvantaged. (i) The Illinois Test of Psycholinguistic Abilities (ITPA) — Grammatical Closure subtest; in this subtest, the child's ability to make use of redundancies in oral language is assessed (Kirk, McCarthy and Kirk, 1968). (ii) The English Picture Vocabulary Test (EPVT) is the British version of the Peabody Picture Vocabulary Test (Brimer and Dunn, 1962) and measures listening vocabulary. The ITPA was administered only to the experimental group at age three. The EPVT was administered to the experimental group at age three and again to the experimental group and the two control groups at age eight.

Cognitive style

The Matching Familiar Figures Test: the subject is presented with pictures of familiar objects (the standard) and asked to choose from six variants the one that is identical to the standard (Kagan, Rosman, Day, Albert and Phillips, 1964). Three scores were calculated: Matching Familiar Figures – latency in response (recorded in seconds); Matching Familiar Figures – number of correct responses; Matching Familiar Figures – number of errors. The test was administered to experimental and both control groups at age eight.

Pre-school achievement

The Preschool Inventory was developed at the Educational Testing Service, Princeton, New Jersey 'to give a measure of achievement in areas regarded as necessary for success in school' (Caldwell, 1967). It has been developed specifically for use with disadvantaged children. Before using the test in Ireland, it was necessary to change the vocabulary of some of the items (elevator, phonograph, gas). One of the 85 questions was omitted altogether (question 29). The test yields four separate scores based on factor analysis as well as a total score. The four factors represented are: A. Personal–Social Responsiveness (information about self – name, parts of body; ability to respond to communications of another person). B. Associative Vocabulary (ability to demonstrate awareness of the connotation of a word to describe the essential characteristics of social roles – policeman, teacher). C_1. Concept Activation–Numerical (ordinal or numerical relations: how many eyes, point to last one). C_2. Concept Activation–Sensory (knowledge of sensory attributes – form, colour, size). The test was administered to the experimental group at ages three and five.

Reading readiness

The Clymer–Barrett Prereading Battery is designed to measure perceptual pre-reading skills (Clymer and Barrett, 1968). The test yields a full-test score and three subtest scores: visual discrimination, auditory discrimination and visual-motor coordination. The test was administered to the experimental group at age six.

Reading attainment

(i) The Marino Graded Word Reading Scale is designed to measure the ability to pronounce correctly English words presented in printed form; reading ages, based on Irish norms are yielded by the scale. Reading quotients were calculated ($\frac{RA}{MA}$ x 100) (O'Suilleabhain, 1970). (ii) Scala Gradaithe sa Gaeilge (Leamh) (1969) is designed to measure ability to pronounce correctly Irish words presented in printed form. Reading quotients ($\frac{RA}{MA}$ x 100) based on the performance of a limited normative sample, were calculated. The two reading tests were administered to experimental and both control groups at age eight.

Personality

Kamii (1971) has suggested teacher ratings as being better suited than tests for the assessment of socio-emotional characteristics of young children. Young children, she argues, are not likely to conceal showing their feelings; besides, information based on daily observation is superior to that based on a short test. The rating scale used in the present study was the Children's Behaviour Rating Scale developed at the Institute for Developmental Studies (nd) at New York Medical College. The scale contains the name, together with a definition of eight traits; each trait is subdivided into five descriptions ranked from high to low ('high' representing a child who possesses the traits to a marked degree) and scaled from 0 to 9. The eight traits are:

(i)   self-determination (extent child takes initiative);
(ii)   persistence (does not give up easily, or is not readily bored or distracted);
(iii)   stimulus-seeking behaviour (curiosity, inquisitiveness);
(iv)   competitiveness (attempts to excel in competition with other children);
(v)   response to direction (dutifully executes requests, commands);
(vi)   dependence (seeks assistance from others);
(vii)   emotional control in situations of failure or frustration (inhibits expression of emotion);
(viii) mood: cheerful — depression (merry, happy, pleasant *vs.* morose, unhappy, gloomy).

The experimental group was rated at age three and at age eight. The two control groups were rated at age eight.

Home environment

The investigations of Dave (1963) and Wolf (1964) indicate that environmental 'process' variables display substantial relationships with measures of achievement and intelligence. These process variables, as distinct from status variables, attempt to describe what parents *do* with children in the home. The instrument used in the present study was the one developed by Dave; adaptations of the instrument were necessary for use with younger children. Mothers of the target children were interviewed by social workers. The home background of each child was assessed in terms of the following variables:

(i)   achievement press — parental aspirations for the education of the child (educational goals);

(ii)   language model — quality of the language usage of parents (pronunciation, vocabulary);

(iii)   academic guidance — extent of general supervision and suggestions regarding school work;

(iv)   family activeness — variety, frequency and educational value of the activities of the family;

(v)   intellectuality of the home — variety and thought-provoking elements in toys and games available to the child;

(vi)   work habits of the family — degree of structure and routine in home management

Information on environmental process variables was obtained for the experimental group at ages three and eight and for both control groups at age eight.

Home status variables

An index of social class based on the father's occupation, was obtained. Each child was assigned to one of five categories: professional, higher administrative and managerial (coded 1), intermediate professional, administrative and managerial (coded 2), skilled (coded 3), partly skilled (coded 4) and unskilled (coded 5) (Great Britain: Registrar General, 1956). Information was also obtained from parents on family size (number of living children in the family). Finally, the target child's ordinal position in family was ascertained. Information on these three home status variables was obtained for the experimental and two control groups at age eight.

Parents' reactions to pre-school

A survey of reactions to the pre-school, largely attitudinal and affective, of a sample of mothers, whose children had attended the school, was carried out. The interview covered:

(i)   mothers' attitudes towards the pre-school;

(ii)   mothers' perceptions of the effects of the pre-school on their children;

(iii)   the extent to which behaviours of the mothers had changed as a result of pre-school contacts;

(iv)   mothers' attitudes towards the junior school (to which children could proceed for three years following their two years in the pre-school).

Only mothers of children who had been members of the experimental group were included in the sample of 25 mothers interviewed. The experimental group had just finished the five-year programme and were aged eight years when the interviews were carried out.

Analyses

The following analyses, the results of which are described in subsequent chapters, were carried out.

1. A description of the characteristics (cognitive, scholastic, perceptual, language, personality and home background) of the experimental group on entering the project at age three is provided in Chapter V.

2. Cognitive and scholastic development of the experimental group during its two years in the pre-school and for the following three years is also described in Chapter V. The description is in terms of general intellectual development, the development of school-related skills and knowledge, and pre-reading and reading skills.

3. On the completion of the project, comparisons are made on a range of cognitive, scholastic, perceptual, language, personality and home background variables between the performance of children who had taken part in the pre-school programme and the performance of non-participating children from disadvantaged and non-disadvantaged backgrounds (Chapter VI). The children were aged eight years at this point.

4. A number of further analyses concern only the experimental group. In these analyses, an attempt is made to relate scholastic performance at age eight to a number of variables: sex of child, pre-school teacher, time of attendance at pre-school (morning or afternoon) and length of stay in experimental programme (Chapter VI).

5. Finally, the reactions of parents (mothers) to the intervention effort are reported (Chapter VII).

Chapter V

Cognitive and Scholastic Development of the Experimental Children

In this chapter, the characteristics of the pre-school children on entering the project are described in terms of their performance on a range of tests of cognitive, perceptual and language abilities and of pre-school achievement. Then the development of the children, during the two years in which they were in attendance at the pre-school, and for the three years following their departure from the pre-school, is described in terms of their general cognitive ability, skills and knowledge related to schooling, and pre-reading and reading skills.

The performance of the children on the final test battery taken at age eight is examined in a later chapter. Here we will be concerned with scores on the Stanford–Binet during the life of the project, scores on the Preschool Inventory taken at age five, the Clymer–Barrett Prereading Tests taken at age six and two reading tests (one in English and one in Irish) which formed part of the final battery. It should be noted that no control group information was available for performance on these tests except those taken in the final battery (the Stanford–Binet and the two reading tests). Thus, many of the comparisons that are made will be related to the normative data for the tests or to the earlier or later performance of the experimental group on the same test.

Characteristics of the pre-school children

On admission to the pre-school, a battery of tests covering cognitive ability, pre-school achievement, perceptual ability (auditory and visual), language and personality was administered to all children (*cf*. Table 4.2). Measures of the children's home environment were also obtained. All children had been in attendance at the pre-school for at least six weeks before they were tested; thus they had some time to adjust to the pre-school and to the conditions of testing. All tests were individually administered.

Means and standard deviations on the cognitive tests are presented in Table 5.1. The mean age of the group at the time of taking the Stanford–Binet Scale, which was administered halfway through the testing programme, was 44 months (SD: 3.7 months). Mean scores for the personality and environmental measures are not given, since no useful comparisons between them and any other data can be made. It will be noted that on most of the cognitive measures, the experimental group scored below the mean. This was so on the Stanford–Binet and on the test of visual-motor integration, on which the group scored five months below the American mean. Mean score on a vocabulary test was also below the norm established for an English population (Brimer and Dunn, 1962). Mean score on another language measure however – the ability to make use of redundancies in oral language (Kirk, McCarthy and Kirk, 1968) – was normal. On measures related to pre-school readiness (which examined the child's fund of information about himself, about social roles as well as about numerical and sensory concepts), the experimental group scored below the norms for both middle class and lower class American children (Caldwell, 1967). Norms were not available for the visual and auditory discrimination inventories. The performance of the group on the Stanford–Binet Scale and the Pre-school Inventory will be discussed in greater detail in a later section. In general, the picture presented by the test results is that of a population that is likely to experience difficulty in school.

Table 5.1: Means and SDs on cognitive tests taken at age 3*
Experimental group (N:90)

	Mean	SD
Stanford–Binet IQ	92.99	13.10
Preschool–Inventory–Personal–Social	9.80	2.88
Preschool–Inventory–Associative Vocab	3.07	2.61
Preschool–Inventory–Numerical Concepts	4.49	2.38
Preschool–Inventory–Sensory Concepts	6.20	3.24
Preschool–Inventory–Total	23.48	8.66
Developm. Test of Visual-Motor Integration Age Equivalent	38.99	6.00
Visual Discrimination Inventory	17.20	9.69
Auditory Discrimination Inventory	29.01	3.55
ITPA – Grammatical Closure Scaled Score	35.90	5.65
English Picture Vocab Test Standard Score	88.98	9.31

* Unless otherwise indicated, raw scores are reported

The intercorrelation matrix for all the variables is given in Table 5.2. An iterative principal factor analysis was performed on this matrix (Kellaghan and Greaney, 1973). Seven factors were identified, of which the first three factors were by far the most important, accounting for three-quarters of the common variance and approximately two-fifths of the total variance. The first had a large cognitive component and may be regarded as reflecting 'general intelligence'. It is best typified by the tasks of the Stanford—Binet Intelligence Scale. In addition, it accounted for nearly one-half of the variance of the Peabody test and the Preschool Inventory Factor C_2. The second factor may be labelled a home environment factor. Five of the six home environment indices loaded highly on it. The third factor was a personality factor with high loadings on four personality ratings — self-determination, persistence, and stimulus-seeking behaviour (all positively) and dependence (negatively). Each of the remaining factors accounted for approximately six per cent of the common variance and only four per cent of the total variance. Two were personality factors, one an auditory factor and one a minor cognitive one.

The emergence of a single environmental factor is surprising. This finding fails to support the differentiation of processes implied in the use of six separate rating measures. It may be that raters formed a general impression of the home that was reflected in all their ratings. However, high intercorrelations between the environmental process variables used in the present study have also been reported in other investigations (Davé, 1963; Kellaghan, 1976b). These findings, together with more formal analyses of the characteristics of the scales (T. Williams, 1975), suggest that the scales may have more limited empirical value than their conceptual differentiation might seem to imply.

The perception by teachers of separate personality traits in children of this age is perhaps even more surprising. Parsons (1959), in dealing with teachers' assessments, has spoken of the presence of a 'moral' component. He sees teachers as evaluating pupils not just in terms of their cognitive learning (information, writing, mathematical thinking), but also in terms of social behaviour (cooperativeness, respect for the teacher) and work-habits. However, he was thinking of older children and in fact speculated that there is a relative lack of differentiation of role in the child starting school. He mentions independence as the most important 'predispositional factor' with which the child enters school. Insofar as one of our factors describes independent behaviour, our data support Parsons' position on the existence of such a trait. However, our findings indicate that teachers are sensitive to a number of attributes that fall into the 'moral' category, even in children as young as three years of age, and so perceive greater differentiation in the personalities

Table 5.2: Intercorrelation matrix of measures on entry to the pre-school (N:90)

	1	2	3	4	5	6	7	8	9	10	11	12	13	14	15	16	17	18	19	20	21	22	23	24
1 Binet IQ																								
2 PS Inv A	43																							
3 PS Inv B	51	45																						
4 PS Inv C_1	51	35	48																					
5 PS Inv C_2	49	51	56	42																				
6 Berry Vis-Perc	47	30	40	39	47																			
7 UCLA Vis Dis	41	39	34	26	40	42																		
8 UCLA Aud Dis	44	32	29	35	38	17	14																	
9 ITPA Gram Clos	46	36	40	50	54	38	41	34																
10 Peabody	60	24	38	41	58	48	31	34	45															
11 Home—Achieve	21	25	26	11	38	17	28	22	19	18														
12 Home—Language	33	37	42	22	42	25	37	37	31	34	71													
13 Home—Acad Guid	28	25	37	23	36	24	31	29	28	25	54	64												
14 Home—Family Act	30	26	39	24	34	25	31	16	27	34	63	61	67											
15 Home—Intell	19	14	26	21	24	25	15	14	27	17	51	49	52	58										
16 Home—Work Habits	06	17	02	09	10	03	09	18	18	18	17	23	18	29	21									
17 Pers—Self-Deter	21	21	24	28	29	25	28	25	27	18	19	23	23	28	11	00								
18 Pers—Persist	36	12	28	36	44	28	25	11	26	23	15	17	23	18	26	03	61							
19 Pers—Stim Seek	39	24	40	40	33	32	38	30	35	35	19	22	32	29	26	11	64	64						
20 Pers—Compet	23	07	23	18	26	26	16	22	13	30	30	23	36	28	22	-02	-04	12	21					
21 Pers—Resp to Dir	27	19	33	33	31	38	10	10	28	13	13	22	37	26	-04	08	34	51	42	10				
22 Pers—Dependence	-24	-13	-26	-40	-22	-21	-32	-32	-24	-23	25	-25	-28	-22	-09	-08	-60	-55	-48	-18	-35			
23 Pers—Emot Cont	22	14	24	27	30	14	22	23	23	20	21	20	18	22	-17	19	34	41	36	06	53	-23		
24 Pers—Mood	-06	14	16	11	02	06	01	-22	02	19	07	21	11	19	-03	24	36	24	26	-25	33	-26	13	

of young children than Parson's position would have led one to expect.

The relative lack of differentiation in cognitive ability revealed in the factor analysis must be regarded as a major feature of our findings. It may be that cognitive ability at this age is relatively undifferentiated (*cf.* Anastasi, 1958) and this may be more true in the case of disadvantaged children than in the case of middle class children. Again, the lack of differentiation may have been a function of the range of the tests selected. Greater differentiation has been reported in a study of three- to five-year-old American children (MacDonald, 1971); in this study, however, measures of more basic perceptual and psychomotor functions were administered. As far as the grouping of higher-order mental functions is concerned, the results of the two studies are not dissimilar.

Since the battery of cognitive tests showed relatively little differentiation among themselves, there seems little value, either in economic or educational terms, in administering such batteries to similar samples of children. The Stanford—Binet Intelligence Scale on its own provides a relatively good estimate of the abilities measured by the cognitive tests used in this study. However, the question must be raised of the appropriateness of the tests we used in terms of tasks and materials for the population being tested. Most of the tests had been designed for use with middle class children and presumably adequately sample the abilities of such children using tasks, materials and processes which are representative of their environments. We cannot be sure that the same is true for children coming from a disadvantaged background. Yet, the use of unfamiliar material may result in children not displaying skills they possess (Kellaghan, 1968). Thus, if the test material used in this study were inappropriate, this could have resulted in masking a differentiation of the skills that may exist in the subjects. Alternative techniques of evaluation will have to be developed before this issue can be resolved.

General cognitive development

The scores of the experimental group on the Stanford—Binet Intelligence Scale show an increase during the period of pre-schooling and then a falling-off for the next three years. Scores and standard deviations at each age level are presented in Table 5.3. In all cases after the first testing, some members of the experimental group were not tested. This was usually because children had moved from the area, though there were a few cases of lack of cooperation in testing by individual children as well as cases in which children were absent from school during the period of testing. For the final testing for the project, at age eight, all children of the original experimental group who were still living in the Dublin area were located and tested. It should be remembered that during the period of the project there was a good deal of movement among some families — in and out of the area and in suburban areas. The location of the sample thus became a problem after the first year. It would have been very expensive and time-consuming to have traced and tested all children each year of the project. At each age level, for children not tested, their mean score on the previous year's testing (when available) was compared with the mean obtained for the whole group in the previous year. Comparisons indicated that the non-tested children were superior in ability to those tested; thus our reported scores do not seem to be biased upwards because of loss from the sample.

Table 5.3: Stanford—Binet IQ scores of experimental group

Age of Testing	N	M	SD
Age 3	90	92.99	13.10
Age 4	85	96.44	12.65
Age 5	68	99.44	13.96
Age 6	82	95.06	13.43
Age 7	75	96.27	10.81
Age 8	85	90.91	11.16

The final test score of 90.91 of the experimental group at age eight may be compared with that of a control group, from the same area, of children of the same age. The mean obtained by the control group was 84.26 (SD: 16.06). One may assume that, without intervention, the mean score of the experimental group could have been of the same order.

It has been argued that the improvement in test scores in longitudinal studies may be a function of the repeated testing to which the group is exposed; in other words, the subjects become test-wise. However, evidence from other longitudinal studies, which examined the developmental profiles of subjects (Sontag, Baker and Nelson, 1958) and which introduced additional subjects who had no previous experience of testing into the testing programme (Freeman and Flory, 1937; Moriarty, 1966), indicates that the cumulative effects of serial testing are slight. Besides, the decline in the Stanford—Binet scores of the experimental group in the present study from the age of five onwards does not support the existence of a practice effect. In the absence of evidence to the contrary, the most likely explanation of the improved performance of the group seems to be their exposure to the pre-school programme.

Variation in intelligence

At this point, it may be worth noting the heterogeneity of the group in terms of intelligence. Even when the programme began and the children were aged three, there was a wide range in their level of intelligence. The lowest IQ score recorded at age three was 59, the highest 125; at age eight, the lowest score was 68 and the highest 128. The range did not change markedly in the intervening years.

The distribution of scores, however, did change somewhat. Table 5.3 indicates that the variance in scores decreased from age three to age eight; the decrease really took place after the children had left the pre-school. Especially during the last two years of the project, there was a tendency for the group to become more homogeneous, though the range of differences even at the final testing is still very considerable.

The series of bar-graphs in Figures 5.1 to 5.4 provide a visual presentation of the distribution of scores on the Stanford—Binet test over four of the occasions on which it was administered. Up to age five, there is an increase in the number of relatively high scores. The number then declines from age six onwards. Whether one takes the cut-off point at just above the mean (101+) or a bit above it (106+), it is clear that the number of children above these cut-off points decreased over the course of the five years. That is, there were less children with 'high' scores at the end of the project than there were at the beginning, with a peak in the centre. Here is at least part of the reason for the reduction in variance.

The question that arises then is do brighter children do less well in the programme than less bright ones? This question is too complex to be answered unequivocally. However, the data we have been looking at, when considered in conjunction with the data for lower scores, suggest that this may be so. The percentage of children with a score of 85 or less was 32 at the age of three. In line with the general upward movement of scores, this figure decreased to 17 per cent at age four, at which level it remains until age six. The next two years witnessed an increase in this percentage — from 23 per cent at age seven to 33 per cent at age eight — a figure similar to that obtained at age three.

A comparison of the distribution of the scores of the experimental

Figure 5.1: Experimental Group — Bar-graph of Stanford—Binet scores age 3 (percentages)

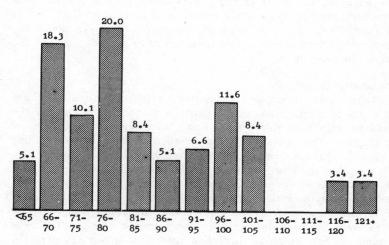

Figure 5.2: Experimental Group — Bar-graph of Stanford—Binet scores age 5 (percentages)

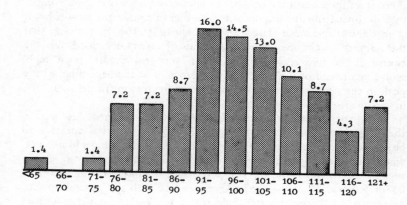

ERRATA

On pages 64 and 65, the captions for
diagrams 1 and 4 have been inadvertently
transposed.

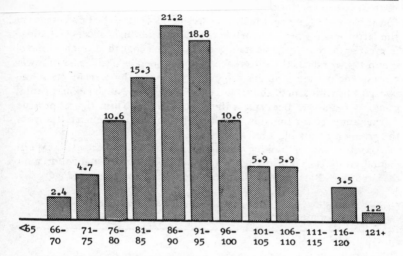

Figure 5.4: Disadvantaged Control Group — Bar-graph of Stanford—Binet scores
age 8 (percentages)

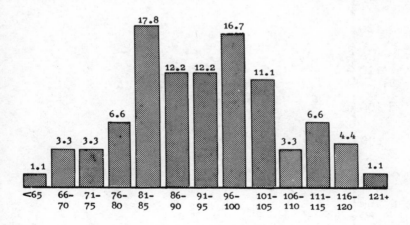

group at age eight with that of the disadvantaged control group at the same age is obtained by examining Figures 5.3 and 5.4. From these it can be seen that there is a marked decrease in the number of low scores in the experimental group as compared with the control group. In the former, while 33 per cent had IQ scores of 85 or less, the percentage for the latter was 62 per cent. While the number of 'high' scores (IQ 106+) is greater in the experimental group (10 per cent) than in the control group (7 per cent), the difference is not as great as in the case of lower scores. The picture is similar when one compares the percentages in the two groups with scores above IQ 100 — 16 per cent of the experimental group as against 15 per cent of the control group. These figures provide further support for the view that brighter children benefitted less from the programme than less bright ones.

Another way of looking at variation in intelligence in the experimental group is to plot the IQ scores obtained by individual children on the Stanford—Binet test at different age levels. The graph in Figure 5.5

Figure 5.5: Regression of Stanford—Binet scores at age 5 on scores at age 3 — Experimental group

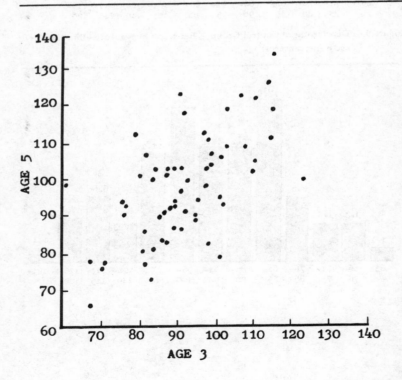

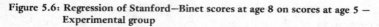

Figure 5.6: Regression of Stanford–Binet scores at age 8 on scores at age 5 — Experimental group

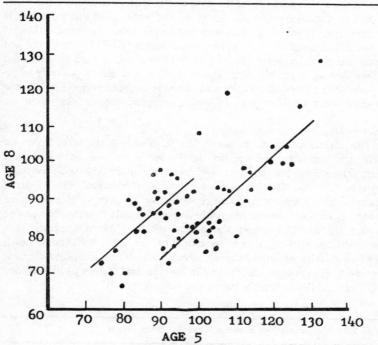

plots scores at the beginning against scores at the end of the pre-school period. An interesting aspect of the display is the number of children who showed very considerable variation in their performance. A child with an IQ below 80 at age three had a score of 114 at age five; another child with a score of 90 at age three obtained a score of 124 at age five. There were also a number of large drops in score — from 124 to 100 and from 102 to 80. Figure 5.6 plots scores at age five against scores at age eight, that is between scores at the time children left the pre-school (and entered a junior school) and scores at the end of the junior school. Cases of extreme variability in scores for individual children occur less frequently than in the case of the previous figure we considered. Such increase in stability is to be expected as the children grow older and is also reflected in the intercorrelations between test scores (*cf.* Table 5.4).

The scatter-gram in Figure 5.6 (five-year-olds and eight-year-olds) differs from that in Figure 5.5 (three-year-olds and five-year-olds) in that in the former there is at least the suggestion of a discontinuity in the regression of the post-test on the pre-test scores (*cf*. Campbell, 1969). Two lines seem to fit the data better than one. The cutting-point occurs at the level of about IQ 94 on the pre-test. If this inference is correct and there is a real discontinuity in the regression, then it appears that children with higher initial scores (IQ 94+) benefitted less from the programme in the long-term than children with lower initial scores (less than IQ 94). Note that this effect was not in evidence when the children were tested at the end of the pre-school period but became apparent over the three years following completion of pre-schooling.

Intercorrelations between testings

The intercorrelations between the Stanford—Binet tests taken on different occasions are set out in Table 5.4. It will be noted that correlations between adjacent age levels are much the same (varying between .75 and .79) irrespective of the ages involved. The reported figures are very similar to those reported for children of this age range based on testings carried out with yearly intervals (Sontag, Baker and Nelson, 1958). The longer the period of time between testings, the lower the correlations; that is, over time the tendency for the individual child to shift in position relative to other children's scores on the test increases. This is a general finding in longitudinal studies of intelligence (*cf*. Pinneau, 1961; Sontag, Baker and Nelson, 1958).

Table 5.4: Intercorrelations between Stanford—Binet scores

	Age 4	Age 5	Age 6	Age 7	Age 8
Age 3	75	63	69	64	56
Age 4		79	79	67	63
Age 5			77	65	68
Age 6				75	73
Age 7					79

The correlation between test performances at ages three and eight (.56) does not provide a very good basis for prediction from test performance at the former age to test performance at the latter age. On the basis of scores at three years of age, only 31 per cent of the variance in test performance at eight years of age can be predicted. There are a number of possible reasons for this. Firstly, there is the possibility of the unreliability of the measure. The test—retest correlation itself is, of course, often taken as an index of reliability. However, we only have figures based on tests administered a year apart. We should expect reliability figures for testings over shorter periods of time to have been higher — a figure of about .90 is reported by McNemar (1942) for intervals of a few weeks. In the absence of short-term reliability figures, measures of internal consistency are of interest. Bayley (1970) reports split-half correlations as high as .95 for tests used with children as young as three years of age. For Stanford—Binet tests in the present study, the following Kuder—Richardson correlations were obtained: at age three, .89; at age four, .86; at age five, .85; at age six, .86; at age seven, .82, and at age eight, .86. These figures are not exceptionally high and certainly leave room for the possibility of inconsistency in the measurement as at least a partial explanation of the intercorrelations reported for the series of retests.

It will be noted, however, that the nearer in time two testings were carried out, the higher the correlation between scores on the two occasions. This suggests there may be factors other than lack of consistency operating. One possibility is that the test is measuring different types of abilities at different ages. At the lower age levels of the Stanford—Binet, there is an apparent difference between items in the amount of verbal content they contain; such content tends to increase with increasing age level. Obviously, if a qualitative change takes place in the ability being measured (McNemar, 1942), performance at one stage might not be a good predictor of performance at a later stage. Another factor that could account for low correlations between one testing and another is the difference in rates of development among the children being tested (Sontag, Baker and Nelson, 1958). The pre-school and early school years are periods of considerable flexibility and it is easy to envisage a child changing his status in intellectual development, relative to other children between the ages of three and eight.

Finally, it is not without significance that here we are speaking of a group of children participating in an experiment. It may be that children reacted differentially to the experimental treatment, which was, of course, the intervention programme. If some children responded more positively than others, then they might have 'benefitted' more, with the result that they could have changed their status relative to other children on the measure of intellectual development used in the study. This, as we have suggested, may have happened in the case of children of different levels of ability.

The pattern of growth of the experimental group

The Stanford—Binet Scale is generally accepted as a measure of 'general intellectual ability' and McNemar's (1942) extensive factor analyses of performance on the scale indicate that performance is largely explicable in terms of a single common factor. However, several attempts have been made to distinguish different abilities that might be tapped by the scale. Since the loadings of items on the general factor vary, one may ask whether different groups of subjects vary in their performances on different types of item. For example, it has been found that for mentally handicapped subjects, the difficulty level is likely to be greater for items with a relatively high loading on the general first factor isolated by McNemar (1942) than for items with a relatively low loading. Thus, handicapped subjects find items like stringing beads, drawing a circle, folding a triangle, reproducing geometric designs and solving factual problems relatively easier than items that involve identifying objects by name and by use, identifying how objects are similar and different and thinking analogically — all items requiring relatively abstract and verbal reasoning (Cruickshank and Qualtere, 1950; Thompson and Magaret, 1947).

There is also evidence that different cultural backgrounds may foster the development of different abilities (e.g., Lesser, Fifer, and Clark, 1965; Porteus, 1939). Eells *et al.* (1951), for example, found that the greatest differences among children from different social classes on a number of intelligence tests occurred in verbal items and the smallest differences in items employing pictures and geometric designs. In the present study, we wish to find out if there are any indications that, on the Stanford—Binet scale, the performance of the experimental group is qualitatively different from that of children from non-disadvantaged backgrounds. In particular, we will be interested in differences on verbal items because of the reported difficulties encountered by children from disadvantaged backgrounds on such items. We will answer the question regarding qualitative differences by comparing the difficulty levels of individual test items for the two groups. Comparisons will be made with the performance of the American standardization sample, since no item statistics are available for an Irish population. This is not an entirely satisfactory procedure, but it may be regarded as acceptable since the mean performance of a normal sample of eight-year-old Irish children on the Stanford—Binet test in the present study was not found to differ much from that of the standardization sample.

The difficulty level and discrimination index of each item in the Stanford—Binet Scale were calculated. The difficulty level is simply the percentage of subjects who passed an item. The discrimination index is the bi-serial correlation between success or failure on an item and total score on the test. Difficulty levels and discrimination indices for the 1960 standardization sample of the Stanford—Binet test are provided in Appendix B of the test manual (Terman and Merrill, 1961).

Before considering comparisons in detail, two general points may be made. Firstly, the statistics on difficulty level in our data, with a few marginal exceptions, show an increase in percentage passing at successive age-levels; such an increase was a factor in the selection of items for the scale in the first instance and is regarded as of major importance in the measurement of a developing function like intelligence (Terman and Merrill, 1961). And secondly, the measures of discrimination for the present sample and for the standardization sample are generally similar with the exception of thirteen indices for the present sample which are very low (less than .40). The explanation for most of these low indices of discrimination is to be found in the fact that the majority of children passed the item; thus discrimination on the basis of performance on the item was not possible. These two factors — decrease in the difficulty of items with increasing age, and the relationship between performance on individual items and the test as a whole — suggest that the subjects of the present investigation are behaving in a similar fashion to the children of the standardization sample in their performance on the Stanford—Binet Scale.

As a general guide towards a classification of different types of item on the Stanford—Binet Scale (which might be indicative of different abilities tapped by the test), Valett's (1965) item classification was used. This is basically a logical classification and is not necessarily discriminative; items categorized under different headings may involve the same or similar processes. Besides, there is obvious overlap between the categories since, in some cases, the same item appears in more than one category. However, the classification seems relevant to some of the discussion regarding the weaknesses of children from disadvantaged backgrounds in some skills and abilities. The classification has six categories: general comprehension (the ability to conceptualize and integrate components into a meaningful total relationship); visual-motor ability (the ability to manipulate materials in problem-solving situations usually requiring integration of visual and motor skills); arithmetical reasoning (the ability to make appropriate numerical associations and deal with mental abstractions in problem solving situations); memory and concentration (the ability to attend and retain; requires motivation and attention and usually measures degree of retention of various test items); vocabulary and verbal fluency (the ability to use words correctly in association with concrete or abstract material; the understanding of words and verbal concepts; the quality and quantity of verbal expression); and judgment and reasoning (the ability to comprehend and respond appropriately in specific situations requiring discrimination, comparison, and judgment in adaptation).

Stanford—Binet items were categorized under the above headings and the difficulty level of each item for our sample was compared with the difficulty level reported by Terman and Merrill (1961) for their standardization sample.* Within each category, only the performance of subjects at the age level for which the item was designated in the test was examined since these are the only statistics provided in the test manual. For example, for an item that appears at the seven-year level in the test, only the percentage of seven-year-olds passing the item was considered. For each item, a simple decision was made: was the item, as indicated by the percentages passing, more difficult for the experimental sample or for the standardization sample? The number of items within each category which was more difficult for the experimental group was then summed; a similar procedure was followed in the case of the standardization sample. It was assumed that if there were no differences between the groups in the abilities represented by the categorization, the number of items within a category which each group would find more difficult than the other group would be approximately half the total number of items in the category.

Of course, by chance one would expect some differences between the groups. The extent to which observed differences are due to chance can be determined from the binomial distribution. Table 5.5 gives the numbers of items for each category which were more difficult for the experimental sample as compared to the standardization sample, together with the number more difficult for the standardization sample as compared to the experimental sample. The associated p-values based on the binomial distribution are also included in the table (Siegel, 1956). (The arithmetic reasoning category is not included as it contains only one relevant item.) The p-values in Table 5.5 indicate that differences between the groups in the numbers of items which one group found more difficult than the other can be attributed to chance.

Table 5.5: Comparison of difficulty levels on items on the Stanford—Binet for the experimental sample and the standardization sample

Category	Total no of items	No. of items more difficult for experi- mental group	No. of items more difficult for standard- ization group	P
General comprehension	10	7	3	.172
Visual-motor ability	12	4	8	.194
Memory & concentration	6	1	5	.109
Vocabulary & verbal fluency	6*	2	3	.500
Judgement & reasoning	20*	12	7	.324

*no difference on one item

* Complete item statistics are contained in Kellaghan (1975).

Our analyses of the performance of the experimental group on the Stanford—Binet Scale suggest that the group, while performing at a somewhat lower level than the standardization sample at all ages except five, do not differ from them in their patterns of response to items on the test. Thus the analyses fail to support the view that the present group of children differ qualitatively from the standardization sample in the nature of their intellectual functioning, such as would have been indicated if, for example, they had found the verbal items consistently more difficult than did the standardization sample. This conclusion requires a qualification. The range of abilities tapped by the Stanford—Binet Scale might be small. If the test, for example, is to be regarded as predominantly measuring a general factor, then Valett's categorization is to some extent spurious and one would not expect differential performance between the groups from category to category. The use of additional tests of a different character to the Stanford—Binet might well show evidence of qualitative differences in ability between our sample and children from non-disadvantaged backgrounds.

Finally, the findings of the present analyses cannot be generalized to other populations living in disadvantaged areas. While such populations can differ in many ways, an obvious difference between the present experimental group and other children from disadvantaged backgrounds is the fact that the experimental group has been involved in a special pre-school programme. The effect of such a programme might have been to change the pattern of abilities of the group. We know that the programme was instrumental in effecting quantitative changes, evidenced in the raising of the mean level of performance of the group on the Stanford—Binet Scale. There also is evidence that children in the area before the project began tended to do less well on tests of a verbal nature relative to a normative sample than on less verbally loaded tests (Kellaghan and Brugha, 1972). The possibility of alteration in qualitative aspects of the intellectual functioning of the group in the present study then cannot be discounted.

Pre-school achievement

The Preschool Inventory is an individual test designed to measure a child's achievement in areas regarded as necessary for success in school. Items on the test are sensitive to experience; because of this, test scores can be taken as indications of deficit in particular areas. Furthermore, they can be used to demonstrate changes associated with educational intervention (Caldwell, 1967). In view of the background of the children and the objectives of the pre-school curriculum in the present project, the test seemed particularly appropriate.

Scores on four 'factors' are yielded by the test: Factor A — Personal—social responsiveness; Factor B — Associative Vocabulary;

Factor C_1 — Concept Activation, Numerical, and Factor C_2 — Concept Activation, Sensory. Mean scores (and standard deviations) on the subtests are presented in Table 5.6 for the experimental group when they took the test at the age of 3 years 8 months. For comparative purposes, the American norms in percentile ranks for each mean are also given. Norms are available for lower class and middle class American samples (Caldwell, 1967). Similar data are provided in Table 5.7 for the group when they took the test two years later; at that time they had completed the pre-school programme and their average age was 5 years 7 months.

Table 5.6: Preschool Inventory: mean scores and SDs for three-year-olds (N: 90)

			Norm (Percentile rank)	
Subtest	M	SD	Lower class	Middle class
A. Personal—Social Responsiveness	9.80	2.88	35	10
B. Associative Vocabulary	3.07	2.61	45	0
C. Concept Activation—Numerical	4.49	2.38	40	20
D. Concept Activation—Sensory	6.20	3.24	35	10
Total	23.48	8.66	35	15

Table 5.7: Preschool Inventory: mean scores and SDs for five-year-olds (N: 62)

			Norm (Percentile rank)	
Subtest	M	SD	Lower class	Middle class
A. Personal—Social Responsiveness	19.86	2.67	60	20
B. Associative Vocabulary	12.45	4.09	65	15
C. Concept Activation—Numerical	12.95	3.04	75	45
D. Concept Activation—Sensory	15.95	2.45	60	5
Total	60.95	10.56	60	5

A clear increase in mean score occurred from the first testing to the second. Of course, without any kind of special intervention, one would have expected an increase over a period of two years. Some indication of whether the increase was greater or lesser than one would have expected without intervention is obtained by looking at the group's position relative to the normative sample. There are problems in using

American data for this kind of comparison — conditions of development may not be the same for children living in a disadvantaged
environment in Dublin as for children living in a disadvantaged
environment in the United States. However, with this reservation in
mind, the normative data are useful in that they give us some anchor
point that we do not otherwise have. From a comparison of the two
tables, it is clear that the experimental group improved their position
relative to the lower class normative group on all subtests. At the
beginning of the project, mean scores on all four subtests were below
the median for the American sample of lower class children of
equivalent age. Two years later, mean scores of the experimental group
on the four subtests are all above the median for the American sample
of the same age. Relative to the American middle class sample, the
experimental group has improved its position on three of the four
subtests but, surprisingly, not on its total score. On all subtests, with
the exception of Concept Activation, Numerical, the experimental
group falls far below the performance of the American middle class
sample. The overall improvement of the experimental group can be
taken as evidence of a programme effect. In the absence of such an
effect, we would have no reason to expect an improved performance on
the part of the experimental group with reference to the performance
of the normative samples.

The improvement in performance over the two-year period of
pre-schooling may be concretely illustrated by reference to some of the
tasks of the Preschool Inventory. For example, the number of children
who could report their own age showed a large increase — from 31 to
82 per cent. The percentages of children who could respond to a series
of verbal instructions also increased — very markedly in some instances.
At the age of three, the only items to which a large number of children
(over 80 per cent) responded were the commands 'Jump' and 'Give
everything (a number of cars and boxes) to me.' By the age of five, the
children were responding to more complex instructions: 'Say "hello"
very softly' (86 per cent), 'Now stand up and face the door' (100 per
cent), 'Put the red car on the black box' (87 per cent) and 'Put three
cars in the big box' (97 per cent). At age three, no child was able to
identify the seasons of the year (the time of the year when it is hottest,
the time of year it is now). A very small percentage (ten per cent or
less) could indicate the way a wheel or a gramophone record turns,
where one buys petrol, what a dentist or what a teacher does.
Somewhat higher percentages knew what a policeman does (14 per
cent), what you would do if you wanted to read something (12 per
cent), and when we eat breakfast (30 per cent). By the age of five all
performances had improved: 72 per cent knew what a policeman does,
66 per cent what to do if you wanted to read something, and 82 per

cent knew when we eat breakfast. However, even after the two years, the number who knew the seasons of the year was still small (less than 28 per cent); these are probably the most abstract items on this section of the test.

Again, at age three, while 40 per cent could rote count to five, only one per cent could actually count the number of toes they had. Where there was a large difference between quantities (two and eight checkers), 41 per cent could indicate which had more and 37 per cent which had fewer. When the number of checkers (six) was equal in two groups, only two per cent denied that one group had not more than the other. The children also had difficulty in indicating the serial position of objects; 37 per cent could point to the 'middle' checker, twelve per cent to the 'first' one, eleven per cent to the 'last one', seven per cent to the 'second' one and two per cent to the 'next-to-last' one.

At the age of five, the increase in the children's ability to manipulate numerical concepts was obvious. Practically all the children (98 per cent) could now rote count to five. Besides, many of them could also apply their numerical ability as evidenced in the success of 97 per cent in indicating how many hands they had; 84 per cent knew how many wheels there were on a car, 87 per cent how many wheels on a bicycle and 97 per cent how many corners on paper. The other aspects of numerical ability tapped by the Preschool Inventory — recognition of differences in quantities and operations involving serial positions — also showed improvement over the two-year pre-school period. When faced with two quantities of checkers, 94 per cent could say in which group there were 'more', only 44 per cent could say in which there were 'fewer' and 52 per cent could recognize when the two groups were equivalent. Serial positions, first (86 per cent), middle (79 per cent) and last (73 per cent), were relatively well coped with. The percentage that could indicate the 'second' of a group of objects however was 50, and the percentage that could indicate the 'next-to-last' position only 39. Thus, while there was a general improvement over the two years, some children were still experiencing difficulty with the more complex concepts in this area.

Finally, the children in the programme also showed considerable improvement in their knowledge of the sensory attributes of objects, such as colour, form, size and motion. On the first testing, as many as 78 per cent passed only one item (drawing a line). On 15 out of 19 items, less than 40 per cent were successful. On the second testing at age five, over 90 per cent of children were successful on nine of the items. On the most difficult item for the group (to identify the colour of night from a series of colours), 63 per cent were successful. This means that the group had considerably increased their knowledge of objects in their physical environment and the properties of such objects

— the shape, colour, size and weight of objects, the speed of objects and similarities between objects.

In conclusion, the evidence from an examination of children's performance on the Preschool Inventory suggests an overall improvement over the two years of the pre-school programme in the areas examined by the test. Some of this improvement, no doubt, is to be attributed to maturational and other factors which were not the direct outcome of the programme. Some of the improvement, however, seems directly attributable to the pre-school programme, which seems to have been most effective in the development of children's knowledge of ordinal and numerical relations. Though it also had some impact in the areas of increasing the child's knowledge of the physical world and the attributes of objects, it seems to have been less successful in increasing knowledge of immediately perceptible sensory attributes (like size, shape, etc.) than of more abstract attributes like the functions of objects. This is not to say that development in the area of sensory knowledge did not take place but rather that it would probably have taken place to the same extent without the programme.

Pre-reading and reading skills

The Clymer—Barrett Prereading Battery is designed to test a child's preparedness for learning to read. More specifically, it sets out to measure the perceptual pre-reading skills and abilities the child has acquired by about the age of six (Clymer and Barrett, 1968). The test yields a full-test score and three subtest scores: visual discrimination (based on letters of the alphabet and words), auditory discrimination (of beginning sounds in words and ending sounds in words) and visual-motor coordination (demonstrated by completion of mutilated geometric shapes and the reproduction of whole words in a sentence). Norms are provided for a not very clearly defined population of children entering the first grade in American schools. No age norms are provided. A reasonable rationale is presented by the authors for the selection of subtests; however, it cannot be claimed that the skills tapped by the subtests are the only relevant ones in learning to read (K. Smith, 1972). On balance, the test is probably no better and no worse than other reading readiness tests (R. Farr, 1972; K. Smith, 1972). It was selected for use in the present study to provide some information on the progress of the subjects of the investigation in learning to read in the fourth year of the study.

Form A of the test was taken by all children towards the end of the first term of their second year in the junior school attached to the pre-school. Thus these children had all spent two years in the experimental school and a little over one year in the junior school. The total number of such children was 58 and their mean age at the time of testing was 6 years 8 months. They were some months older than the children for whom norms were available. The test is a group test and was administered to the children in their own classrooms.

Table 5.8 sets out the mean raw scores (and standard deviations) of the experimental children on each subtest as well as for the total test. Equivalent stanine scores based on the American norms are also provided. (In converting to stanine scores, the mean is set at 5 and the standard deviation at 2.) It will be noted that mean stanines of the experimental children on two of the subtests and on the total are all within a standard deviation of the mean. The visual discrimination subtest score was one stanine above the mean, the auditory discrimination subtest score one stanine below the mean and the total score was at the mean. Clymer and Barrett (1968) regard stanine scores of 4, 5 or 6 as indicating adequate development of the skill. Performance on the visual-motor coordination subtest was poorer than in the case of the other subtests. The mean stanine score for the group was 3, which is a standard deviation below the mean. Such a score, according to Clymer and Barrett indicates a minimal preparation in and development of the skills measured.

Table 5.8: Mean scores and stanine equivalents on the Clymer—Barrett pre-reading battery

Subtest	M	SD	STANINE EQUIVALENT OF MEAN
Visual discrimination	39.70	12.13	6
Auditory discrimination	24.40	11.26	4
Visual-motor coordination	10.02	6.83	3
Total	71.26	27.20	5

In terms of the item content of the test, we may say that the ability of the children to recognize the letters of the alphabet and to match words containing from three to six letters was relatively good. Likewise their ability to discriminate sounds at the beginning and ends of words was not unsatisfactory. When the items assume a motor component however (such as is involved in the completion of geometric shapes and the copying of words), performance is notably less satisfactory. These items, of course, involve the ability to write as well as testing the child's ability to analyze complex visual patterns.

Overall, the performance of the children on the early reading skills measured by the Clymer—Barrett test are reasonably satisfactory. The comparisons with the normative sample are fairly stringent since the normative group was a normal population of subjects. Thus, no allowance is made for the disadvantaged background of our subjects. Our subjects did, however, have some advantages. They were somewhat older than the average child entering the first grade in an American school on whom the norms are based. They also probably had more experience of schooling which may have been helpful in developing test-taking skills, such as following the directions of a test administrator.

The large standard deviation associated with the scores indicates that the progress of all children was not satisfactory. On the visual discrimination subtest, for example, while no children had less than 10 of the 55 items correct, three had 12 or less items correct — a raw score which gave them stanine scores of two. On the auditory discrimination task, two children had no item correct (out of 40 items), a further eleven had raw scores that gave them stanine scores of one. As one would expect from the mean scores, the number of low scores on the visual motor coordination subtest was greatest. Five children failed to score; a further five had a score of two or three (out of 27 items). All of these children were assigned stanine scores of one. The number obtaining a stanine score of two was seventeen.

If there were low scores, there also were very high ones. Six children had a score of 54 or 55 (out of a possible 55) on the visual discrimination subtest giving them stanine scores of nine. Ten children obtained scores of 39 or 40 (out of a possible 40) on the auditory discrimination subtest, again earning stanine scores of nine. No child earned a perfect score (27) on the visual motor coordination subtest, providing further evidence of the difficulty of the tasks in this subtest for the children in the study. Two children, however, with raw scores of 24, achieved stanine scores of eight. These contrasts in scores again serve to underline the heterogeneity of the children in the study.

If the Clymer—Barrett test could be taken as measuring all the skills involved in the early learning of reading, then the situation of the subjects in the present study could be regarded as reasonably satisfactory. One might expect something like an average performance in reading from the group in the following years. However, as we have already indicated, we have no guarantee that other factors are not involved in the development of reading skills. Correlations quoted by Clymer and Barrett (1967) between scores on their test and measures of reading ability (subtests of the Stanford Achievement Tests, the Gates Primary Reading Test, the Gates—MacGinitite Reading Tests and the Metropolitan Achievement Test) at the end of the first grade vary between .40 and .69. In no case can more than 50 per cent of the variance in reading scores be predicted. This obviously leaves room for the operation of other factors.

We may anticipate the results of the reading test taken by our subjects at age eight at this juncture, since it seems appropriate to consider them in the light of the children's performance on the Clymer—Barrett test. It was suggested above that the Clymer—Barrett results gave no reason for not expecting normal progress in the development of reading in the group. However, this expectation was not to be fulfilled.

At age eight, the Marino Graded Word Reading Scale (O Suilleabhain, 1970) was administered as part of a battery of scholastic tests to children in the experimental group. The test measures word recognition, or more precisely, the ability to pronounce correctly English words presented in printed form. There are ten words at each age level from five through fifteen and a further ten words at each age level from sixteen through nineteen. The test has been standardized on an Irish population. For the present study it had the disadvantage that it might not discriminate very well at the level of reading ability of the children in the sample, since one would expect these children to score at the lower end of the scale.

A test of Irish reading attainment, Scala Gradaithe sa Gaeilge (Leamh, 1969), which is similar in format to the Marino Word Reading Scale was also administered at age eight. The test is designed to measure ability to pronounce correctly Irish words presented in printed form. It consists of ten words at each age level from seven through twelve. The test was standardized on a limited sample. From the point of view of the present study, the test suffers from the same disadvantage as the Marino Graded Word Reading Scale in that it might not be expected to discriminate very well at the level of Irish reading ability of children in the sample. However, no other standardized test of Irish attainment was available.

Irish was not a part of the pre-school programme; however on entering junior school, the children, in common with other Irish school children, commenced the study of Irish. For all the children in our sample, Irish would, of course, have been a second language. It is unlikely that their parents would have had any but the most superficial knowledge of the language.

The mean reading age of the experimental group on the Marino Word Reading Scale at age eight was 6.78 years (SD: 1.53)*; the mean

---

* There is a danger that 'reading age' scores will be reified and that interpretations will be attached to the scores which are not justified. For this reason the *Standards for Educational and Psychological Tests* (American Psychological Association, American Educational Research Association, National Council on Measurement in Education, 1974) discourage their use. No special significance is attached to the reading age scores in this study.

reading quotient was 79.18 (SD: 18.50). The mean reading age on the Irish test was somewhat higher: 7.52 years (SD: 0.78). The mean reading quotient was 87.13 (SD: 8.56). These figures may be contrasted in Table 5.9 with the scores of a control disadvantaged and a control non-disadvantaged group. The experimental group performed no better than the disadvantaged control group on the English reading test. On the Irish reading test, their performance was superior. Both groups from disadvantaged backgrounds scored over a standard deviation below the control group from non-disadvantaged backgrounds.

Table 5.9: Means and SDs on reading tests: experimental (n: 85), disadvantaged control (n: 60) and non-disadvantaged control (n: 60) groups

Measure	Experimental		Control disadvantaged		Control non-disadvantaged	
	M	SD	M	SD	M	SD
English RQ	79.18	18.50	79.00	17.58	103.58	16.12
Irish RQ	87.13	8.56	83.25	10.95	107.76	11.33

It will be noted that the variance on the Irish test is considerably smaller than on the English test. This was at least partly due to the fact that the range of possible lower scores on the Irish test was more limited than on the English test, a fact that is reflected in the number of children who received the lowest possible score on the two tests (the figure for the Irish test was 37, while that for the English test was 15). All these children failed to pronounce correctly even one word on the test.

At the other end of the scale some children received quite high scores. One child had a reading age of 13.1 years on the English reading test; 15 others had reading age scores of 10.0 years or more. On the Irish test, one child obtained a reading age score of 13.3; 14 others had reading age scores of 10.0 years or more. Once again, we are reminded of the heterogeneity of the group in terms of their attainments. Obviously, the performance of those children with reading age scores of ten years or more is quite satisfactory. On the other hand, there is also a large number of children with extremely poor reading performance. In general (when one considers mean scores), the reading attainments of the experimental group cannot be regarded as satisfactory.

There are difficulties in comparing performance on the pre-reading test with later reading attainment. However, it does seem clear that the

performance of the group, relative to normative data, at the level of
initial reading (at age six) was more satisfactory then performance two
years later, when that performance is compared to admittedly different
normative data. If one can extrapolate from these comparisons, then it
would appear that the reading development of the group fell off during
the junior school period between the ages of six and eight.

Another way of looking at the relationship between performance on
the pre-reading tests and later reading attainment is to look at
intercorrelations between test scores. These intercorrelations are presented in Table 5.10. The table also contains correlations between
subtests on the pre-reading test; these are of a similar order to those
reported by Clymer and Barrett (1967); if anything, there is a tendency
for ours to be higher.

Table 5.10: Intercorrelations between pre-reading tests (age 6) and reading tests
(age 8) (N: 58)

	1	2	3	4	5
1. Pre-reading—visual discrimination					
2. Pre-reading—auditory discrimination	51				
3. Pre-reading—visual motor coordination	58	65			
4. Pre-reading—total	88	81	76		
5. Marino Reading Age	57	52	36	62	
6. Irish Reading Age	51	44	43	57	80

The high correlation between scores on Irish reading and on English
reading (.80) is also a feature of the table. This correlation indicates
that the skills measured by the two tests have a good deal in common;
obviously skills of decoding, manipulation of symbols and perceptual
analysis, even though the match between grapheme and phoneme may
vary from language to language, are relevant in the reading of any
language. The 'skills of literacy' are common to all languages, and once
acquired, do not have to be learned again (Mountford, 1970). It is of
interest that the children in the present investigation began the study of
Irish about a year later than is normal for Irish school-children, with no
obvious disadvantage as far as their Irish reading was concerned. By
comparison with children of similar age, living in the area before the
establishment of the pre-school, their performance on Irish reading was
superior.

Correlations between the subtests of the pre-reading scale and later
performance on English reading are rather similar to correlations
between the pre-reading subtests and Irish reading. The magnitude of

correlation varies between .36 and .57. On the whole, these are not dissimilar to the predictive correlations cited by Clymer and Barrett (1968). It is of interest that Stanford—Binet IQ scores at age six predict reading attainment at age eight as well as any of the individual subtests of the pre-reading battery. The correlations between the total score on the pre-reading battery and later reading attainment scores were higher than the correlations between subtest scores and later reading attainment (.62 for English and .57 for Irish). Of the individual subtests, visual discrimination had the highest correlations with later reading attainment. This subtest involves recognition of letters and the matching of words. As has been found in other studies (Silberberg, Iversen and Silberberg, 1968; Telegdy, 1975), this finding indicates that, among pre-reading skills, letter knowledge is the best predictor of later reading attainment. However, it seems that letter-naming ability involves a variety of skills -- visual perception, manipulation and abstract reasoning as well as familiarity with letters (Telegdy, 1974).

The level of all the predictive correlations indicates that, in addition to the skills tapped by the pre-reading test and the intelligence test, other factors affect a child's later performance in reading. No doubt some of these factors are related to the reading instruction programme which the child is exposed to; others are probably to be found in the child's own values, attitudes, motivations and aspirations, which to some extent at any rate are most likely a function of the values, attitudes, motivations and aspirations of his out-of-school environment.

Conclusion

Several conclusions emerge from our series of analyses designed to throw light on the cognitive development of the experimental group between the ages of three and eight years. Firstly, there was an increase in IQ scores from the age of three (mean: 92.99) to the age of five (mean: 99.44). This was followed by a steady decline up to the age of eight (mean: 90.91) when the group stood at about the same position on the Stanford—Binet test as when they were three years of age. This trend is similar to that reported in several studies of children from disadvantaged backgrounds carried out in the United States. However, while many of the American studies report no difference between children who had gone through a pre-school programme and control children who had not, when tested at a later age, this is not the finding of the present investigation. The experimental group in our study at age eight was significantly different in intelligence from a control group of children from the same area. The assumption is that, without intervention, the IQ level of the experimental subjects would have dropped even further during their school years. The fact that the children had not lost their position on the Stanford—Binet Scale at age eight, relative to their standing at age three, is interpreted as an effect of the pre-school intervention programme.

A second conclusion from the analyses relates to the performance of the more able and less able children. During the two years of the pre-school, children at all levels seemed to gain from the programme. However, in the post–pre-school period, the regression to the mean on the Stanford–Binet was greater among the 'brighter' children than among the less bright. The number of children with relatively high scores decreased while the number with relatively lower scores remained about the same. A comparison of scores of the experimental group with the scores of the control group at age eight and the evidence from the scatter-grams of the regression of scores of the experimental group at age eight on scores at age five add further weight to the inference that brighter children benefitted less from the pre-school programme than less bright ones. This finding casts doubts on conclusions (e.g. Bronfenbrenner, 1974) that brighter children benefit more from pre-school intervention programmes than less bright ones. At least within the range of measured ability of the children who participated in the present programme, this was not found to be so. The reason for this phenomenon may lie outside the school. Wiseman (1967, 1968) has claimed that adverse environmental conditions have a greater effect on brighter children than on the less able. If this is so, special consideration may need to be given to the potentially more able child when planning intervention programmes (*cf.* Gallagher, 1968).

A consideration of the intercorrelations between testings on the Stanford–Binet scale at different points in time indicates that there was considerable movement in the scores of the children. Thirty-one per cent of the variance in IQ scores at age eight is predictable from scores at age three. A consideration of errors of measurement arises here. However, it also seems that there is considerable variation in, and flexibility for, cognitive development between the ages of three and eight.

There have been many statements which suggest that qualitative differences in cognitive abilities exist between children from disadvantaged and children from non-disadvantaged backgrounds. A comparison of the performance of the experimental group on clusters of items on the Stanford–Binet Scale with the performance of the population on which the test had been standardized did not provide any evidence of qualitative differences between the groups. While overall, the experimental group did less well than the normative sample on the test, there were no indications that this poorer performance was due to weaknesses in particular areas like general comprehension, vocabulary or verbal fluency. It is not possible to say whether this is true of children from disadvantaged backgrounds in general or is true only following an intervention programme of the type to which the subjects of this investigation had been exposed.

In terms of children's knowledge about their world, their vocabulary and concepts (numerical and sensory), as measured by the Preschool Inventory, the experimental group in the present study revealed many weaknesses when assessed at the age of three. When their performance was compared with that of a normative sample from lower social backgrounds in the United States, the experimental group did less well on all subtests of the Inventory. Their performance relative to middle class norms was of course even poorer. At the end of two years in the pre-school (at age five), the experimental group surpassed the normative lower class sample on all subtests. They also improved their position relative to the middle class normative sample in their knowledge of their own personal world, in their ability to respond to verbal communication, in their vocabulary (knowledge of the meaning, attributes and functions of objects and events) and in their knowledge of numerical concepts (knowledge of ordinal or numerical relations). Despite the fact that the experimental group had considerably increased their knowledge of the sensory attributes of objects (colour, form, size and motion), they did not increase their position relative to the middle class norms.

Our final conclusions relate to the development of reading skills. On a pre-reading test (Clymer—Barrett), which the children took at the age of six and a half years, their performance on tests of visual discrimination (involving the recognition of letters of the alphabet and the matching of words) and auditory discrimination (involving the discrimination of sounds at the beginning and end of words) seemed satisfactory in terms of the American norms. Performance on tasks of visual-motor co-ordination (the completion of geometric shapes and the copying of words) was relatively poor.

At the age of eight, the performance of the experimental group on a test of word recognition in English was no better than that of a disadvantaged control group, who had been tested before the introduction of the experimental programme. Performance on Irish reading was, however, superior to that of the control group. When compared to a non-disadvantaged control group, the performances of both the experimental and control disadvantaged groups on the two reading tests were more than a standard deviation below the norm.

It will be noted that the poorer performance of the experimental group occurred after they have left the pre-school. After an initial boost in performance during the pre-school period, manifested in scores on the Stanford—Binet Intelligence Scale, the Preschool Inventory, and probably reflected also in the pre-reading test battery, the performance of the group went into decline. This was clear on the Stanford—Binet

Scale and probably also occurred in reading skills.

Does this pattern of results mean that it is possible to raise the level of ability during the pre-school years but that it is more difficult to maintain that increase from the age of six onwards? The evidence from American studies would seem to indicate that this is indeed true. However, it is also important to bear in mind that intervention at the pre-school level has generally been more intensive, better organized and based on a more solid rationale than intervention during the years of formal schooling. Such was certainly the case in the present study. The importance of the need for improving the kind of provision made for children from disadvantaged backgrounds during the primary school years is an inescapable conclusion of the findings we have been considering.

Chapter VI

Performance at Eight Years of Age

We have already seen something of the performance of the group of children who had taken part in the experimental pre-school programme when they reached the age of eight years. In particular, we considered their performance on the Stanford—Binet Intelligence Scale and their reading attainment. In this chapter, we examine their performance on a wider range of variables. In so doing, we shall first of all compare their performance with that of a group of eight-year-old children who had been living in the area prior to the introduction of the intervention programme. In a second comparison, the performance of a group of children living in non-disadvantaged environments is added. Since local normative data were not available for most of the tests used in the study, information was obtained on performance on the tests for a small representative sample of children in the city in which the project was based. (This is called the non-disadvantaged control group.) Thus, three groups are involved in the comparisons and two sets of comparative analyses were carried out, providing information on how the experimental group stands relative to children from a disadvantaged background who have not taken part in a pre-school programme as well as relative to a normal population. Having considered the performance of the experimental group in relation to the performance of other groups, we shall then turn to a consideration of the performance of sub-groups within the experimental group itself. Here we shall look at the performances of boys and of girls, the performances of children taught by different teachers, the effects of morning attendance as against afternoon attendance, and the relationship between performance and length of stay in the experimental programme.

The variables on which groups were compared were described in Chapter IV (cf. Table 4.2 in particular). It will be noted that information was available for comparisons on variables in the areas of cognitive, perceptual, language and scholastic development, as well as on the personalities and home backgrounds of children.

Several statistical procedures were employed in analyzing data. For each individual variable, an analysis of variance was carried out to test the significance of differences in performance between groups. Carrying out separate analyses in this way has the disadvantage that many of the analyses may be telling us basically the same thing, since the performance of subjects on the different variables used in the analyses are known to be interrelated. For this reason, an alternative method of analysis (multivariate analysis of variance) was also employed. In this approach, all dependent variables are entered in a single analysis and, in the estimation of differences between groups, interrelationships between variables are taken into account. Thus, the method permits an examination of the significance of *overall* differences between groups. If overall differences between group performances are found to exist, we can go a step further and attempt to describe the main dimensions of such differences. This is done through discriminant function analysis, a special type of factor analysis, which reduces the dimensionality of data and allows one to identify and display the test variables that contribute most to differentiation between groups.*

Mean scores and standard deviations on all variables for the experimental and two control groups are presented in Table 6.1. Before contrasting the performance of the experimental group with that of the other groups, we may note that the performance of the control group from the disadvantaged background was consistently inferior to that of the group living in non-disadvantaged environments on a range of scholastic and home measures. Thus, earlier evidence from this country and from elsewhere relating to the scholastic performance of children in disadvantaged backgrounds was confirmed and the need for the present investigation justified.

Experimental versus disadvantaged control group

A comparison of the performances of the experimental and disadvantaged control groups revealed significant differences between the groups. This was true whether one used a univariate or a multivariate method of analysis. On the univariate analyses, significant

---

* For a description of the multivariate techniques used in these analyses cf. Cooley and Lohnes, 1962, 1971; Bock and Haggard, 1968; Lohnes, 1966; Tatsuoka, 1970, 1971; Woodward and Overall, 1975. The programme used for multivariate analysis of variance is described in *OSIRIS III, volume 1: System and program description*. Ann Arbor, Michigan: Inter-University Consortium for Political Research, University of Michigan, 1973. The programme for the discriminant function analysis is contained in NIE, N.H., HULL, C.H., JENKINS, J.G., STEINBRENNER, K., and BENT, D.H. (1975). *Statistical Package for the Social Sciences*, 2nd ed. New York: McGraw-Hill.

Table 6.1: Means, SDs: experimental (n: 82), disadvantaged control (n: 56) and non-disadvantaged control (n: 58) groups

TEST	Experimental		Disadvantaged control		Non-disadvantaged control	
	M	SD	M	SD	M	SD
Stanford–Binet IQ	91.32	10.97	84.71	16.49	105.31	10.80
Cattell Culture Fair IQ	91.78	15.82	100.32	15.34	107.29	12.62
English Picture Vocab	77.24	9.73	73.29	11.69	84.83	8.55
Visual–Motor Integration	78.63	17.12	81.10	14.92	97.97	18.03
Matching Fam. Fig: Latency	8.77	4.49	12.13	6.40	14.84	6.94
Matching Fam. Fig: No correct	4.13	1.76	4.45	2.26	5.52	2.42
Matching Fam. Fig: No errors	16.54	5.73	14.18	6.13	12.00	6.26
English RQ	79.56	18.55	79.63	17.99	103.81	16.42
Irish RQ	87.30	8.67	83.34	11.03	107.86	11.40
Social class	4.17	0.93	4.34	0.90	3.02	1.03
Family size	5.77	2.83	6.09	2.89	4.34	1.75
Ordinal position	3.93	2.91	4.05	2.31	3.02	1.68
Home: achievement press	28.27	6.66	24.29	7.64	37.22	8.80
Home: language	9.33	2.33	7.25	2.40	10.66	2.81
Home: academic guidance	12.82	3.24	9.95	4.09	15.88	3.37
Home: activities	13.88	3.19	12.21	4.49	18.93	4.70
Home: intellectuality	6.35	2.06	6.02	2.29	10.22	2.81
Home: work habits	8.72	2.71	6.79	3.01	9.28	2.73
Pers: self determination	5.17	2.37	5.02	2.68	5.74	1.77
Pers: persistence	5.23	2.29	5.10	2.49	5.92	1.65
Pers: stimulus seeking	3.99	2.76	3.58	3.11	4.71	2.50
Pers: competitiveness	4.24	2.26	4.30	2.84	5.50	2.27
Pers: response to direction	6.07	2.73	6.30	3.04	7.05	2.13
Pers: dependence	4.80	2.14	5.23	2.13	4.61	2.20
Pers: emotional control	6.11	2.48	6.57	2.72	7.15	1.59
Pers: mood	6.55	2.37	6.87	2.74	8.00	1.17

differences in favour of the experimental group were found on the Stanford—Binet IQ and the English Picture Vocabulary Test (both measures of verbal ability), on Irish reading and on five of the six home process variables. Significant differences in favour of the control group were found on the Cattell Culture Fair Test and on two of the measures derived from the Matching Familiar Figures — Mean Latency and Number of Errors. The differences between the groups on other variables (which include all the personality variables) were not statistically significant. The fact that no difference was found between the groups for social class, family size or ordinal position in family was to be expected, since both groups were drawn from the same neighbourhood.

In the discriminant analysis, the single function that emerged from the measurement battery as providing optimal discrimination between the groups was heavily weighted by intelligence (Table 6.2). Verbal intelligence received a high positive weight and non-verbal intelligence a high negative weight. Other high positive weights were attached to home environment measures relating to the language and academic guidance of the home and to reading. A child who had been through the experimental programme differed from one who had not, in that he was likely to score higher on the Stanford—Binet test; furthermore, his home was likely to be rated more highly in terms of the general quality of the language and language models used by parents, in the opportunities for the use of, and enlargement of, vocabulary and sentence patterns, in the keenness of the parents for correct and effective use of language, in the availability of guidance on matters relating to school work and in the availability and use of materials and facilities related to school learning.

In the light of other differences between groups, the failure to find any differences on the personality measures is surprising. True, the main focus of the pre-school programme was not on personality development; however, it was not ignored and one might have expected the additional school experience of the experimental group to have had some effect on such characteristics as the curiosity, inquisitiveness, initiative and persistence of the children. If such effect did occur, it was not perceived by the teachers who rated the children.

There were a number of tests on which the experimental group performed less well than the disadvantaged control group. A relatively high score on the measure of cognitive style (in terms of latency — i.e., time taken to respond — and a low number of errors) is a characteristic of the disadvantaged control group rather than of the experimental group. The disadvantaged control group originally performed as well as the non-disadvantaged control group on the latency measure; this may have been because the reflective attitude of children of low socio-

Table 6.2: Discriminant function coefficients: experimental versus disadvantaged control: main loadings

Variable	Weight
Stanford-Binet IQ	.19
Home: language	.11
Home: academic guidance	.11
Irish Reading Quotient	.08
Matching Familiar Figures: Mean Latency	−.10
English Reading Quotient	−.12
Cattell IQ	−.19
Group	*Centroids*
Experimental	.18
Disadvantaged control	−.27

economic status relative to middle class ones improves by the age of eight (*cf.* Kaplan and Mandel, 1969). If this is so, it helps to explain the good performance of the disadvantaged control group, but not the poor performance of the experimental group. Is the latter to be interpreted as meaning that children who have taken part in the experimental programme are less reflective and more impulsive than children who have not had such an experience? Does this, in turn, mean that they have lower anxiety over failure (Kagan, 1967)?

When the Matching Familiar Figures Test was selected for inclusion in the present study, it was in the belief that reflection-impulsivity could be operationalized in terms of decision time under conditions of uncertainty which the test provided. At the time, it was also assumed that impulsivity was related to wider personality characteristics, the impulsive child being characterized as restless, easily distractable, emotionally uncontrolled and aggressive (Block, Block and Harrington, 1974). As has been pointed out more recently, however, 'it is a heavy responsibility for one measure (or simple variants of the measure) to be taken as the sole and sufficient criterion of impulsive and reflective behaviour' (Block *et al.*, 1974). It is an even more heavy responsibility to regard the measure as indicative of a wide range of other personality measures. The implications of Latency and Error scores on the Matching Familiar Figures Test is at present a matter of controversy (Block *et al.*, 1974, 1975; Kagan and Messer, 1975), the value of the former appearing to be particularly ambiguous. In the present investigation, comments of the testers suggest that the response rate of the experimental group reflected a less inhibited and more confident attitude (less anxiety?) on their part in the test situation. Their feeling, however, was that the shorter latency time recorded was not to be interpreted as reflecting a generalized tendency on the part of children not to consider and evaluate alternatives in a decision-making situation — a feeling supported by the findings of Block *et al.* (1974). In the light of present evidence, observed differences between the experimental and control groups cannot be interpreted as indicating differences in a general trait of impulsivity.

Accuracy scores on the Matching Familiar Figures test seem to be more easily interpretable than Latency scores. Block *et al.* (1974) note a tendency for Accuracy scores to correlate positively with measures of intelligence, a tendency that also appears in our findings. For example, we found that the correlations between Accuracy scores and scores on the Stanford—Binet and Cattell tests ranged between .41 and .49. A correlation of the same order was obtained between the Matching Familiar Figures Test and the Visual-Motor Integration Test. These correlations indicate that the ability reflected in the Matching Familiar Figures Test Accuracy and Errors scores is at least in part a perceptual—intellectual one. Kagan's (1965) descriptions of the test as involving complex visual discrimination tasks supports this view.

The difference between experimental and control groups, in favour of the latter, on the Cattell Culture Fair Test of Intelligence also requires some comment. While it is probably true to say that the main focus of the pre-school programme was verbal—cognitive rather than non-verbal—cognitive, and while one might not have expected such a programme to raise the performance of participants on relatively non-verbal tests, at the same time, one would hardly have expected that it would have had the effect of depressing scores relative to those of children who had not participated in the programme. Perhaps a strong emphasis on verbal development does have this effect; our present data cannot resolve the issue. In passing, it may be noted that the scores of the disadvantaged control group on the Cattell test were rather high. In fact, their mean score (100.32) was the equivalent of the mean of the American standardization sample; this is quite out of line with their scores on other tests. It may be that this was an unusual score and not representative of children living in the area. Findings from another study (McGee, 1970) on the performance of children in the area on somewhat similar tests (the Raven's Matrices and the performance section of the Wechsler Intelligence Scale for Children) indicate that the mean score on the Cattell intelligence scale achieved by the disadvantaged control group in the present study is not typical of the performance of children in the area.

Experimental versus disadvantaged control versus non-disadvantaged control group

Between-group differences become more apparent when one includes in the comparative analyses the performance of the non-disadvantaged control group. In univariate analyses of variance, in which the performances of the experimental and two control groups are considered simultaneously, all differences between groups were statistically significant (many of them highly so), with the exception of three of the personality measures. The only personality variables on which differences were significant were..the measures of competitiveness, emotional control and mood; on all of these, the children from non-disadvantaged backgrounds scored highest. The multivariate analysis of variance also revealed overall differences between groups. Furthermore, significant differences were found to exist between all pairs of the three groups involved in the comparison.*

Two functions were identified in the discriminant analysis. The first (which is considerably more important than the second in that 72.8 per cent of the explained variance is attributable to it) has a large attainment component (Table 6.3). Attainment variables and home variables weight heavily on it, while personality measures do not figure as contributing much. The three groups are clearly separable in terms of this function. The non-disadvantaged control children do best; there is a considerable gap between their performance and that of the experimental group whose level of performance falls between that of the two control groups. Thus, while the experimental subjects do better than the disadvantaged control group, they do not approach the level of children from a non-disadvantaged area in their performance.

The second function is largely an intelligence function on a verbal—non-verbal ability dimension. The largest positive weights are attached to non-verbal intelligence and two home process variables, covering family activeness (extent and content of indoor and outdoor activities of the family, use of TV, books, periodicals etc.) and achievement press (parental aspirations for the education of the child, press for academic activities, knowledge of child's progress at school, planning for attainment of educational goals). The largest negative weights are attached to scores on the Stanford—Binet IQ and two other home variables, one of which relates to the language of the home (quality of language usage of parents, opportunities for use and enlargement of vocabulary and sentence patterns) and the other to academic guidance (availability of guidance on matters relating to school work, availability and use of materials and facilities related to school learning). One can see how these latter home variables are likely to be associated with verbal ability as measured by the Stanford—Binet

---

* F-ratios associated with Hotelling's T^2 were used to examine differences between pairs of groups (Rulon and Brooks, 1968).

Intelligence Scale. One can also see how certain aspects of family activeness (such as use of TV and involvement in outdoor activities) might not be so closely related to the development of verbal skills. While in general one would expect achievement press to be related to intellectual development, unrealistic aspirations on the part of parents might not have that effect.

Table 6.3: First discriminant function coefficients: experimental versus disadvantaged control versus non-disadvantaged control: main loadings

Variable	Weight
English Reading Quotient	.45
Cattell IQ	.30
Home: language	.24
Visual motor integration	−.25
Home: family activeness	−.29
Home: Intellectuality	−.31
Irish Reading Quotient	−.90

Group	Centroids
Non-disadvantaged control	−1.26
Experimental	.43
Disadvantaged control	.68

The second function also differentiates clearly between the groups. The disadvantaged control group score at the non-verbal end of the function, the experimental group in an intermediate position and the non-disadvantaged control group at the verbal end of the function.* It is interesting to note that the discriminant function analysis was successful in distinguishing what is primarily an 'attainment function' and what is primarily an 'intelligence' function. It is also interesting that when the variance relating to the first function has been removed, the experimental group do well on tests of verbal intelligence.

---

* This order can present some difficulties when the mean scores obtained by the groups on variables loading highly on this function (Cattell IQ, achievement press of the home) are considered (Table 6.2). However, it should be recalled that the second discriminant function is concerned with revealing the dimension along which the largest group differences exist *which have not been accounted for* by the first function. Since the two functions are uncorrelated with one another, the weights attached to the variables of the second function refer to variance that is 'left over' in those variables after variance relevant to the first function (in this case 'attainment') has been taken up.

Performance within the experimental group

In this section, we will look at the performance of a number of sub-sets of the experimental group, since it is possible that differences in performance, which are associated with identifiable characteristics of sections of the group, exist. In Chapter V, we saw some evidence to support the view that bright children in the experimental programme did less well than less bright children on the Stanford—Binet Intelligence Scale. Here we will consider performance on the whole range of measures obtained on the children at age eight (cognitive, attainment, personality and home background) and the methods of analyses will be similar to those used earlier in this chapter — analysis of variance (univariate and multivariate) and discriminant function analysis. We shall look first at a personal characteristic (sex) and then at a number of aspects of participation in the programme. The performance of children who had attended the morning session will be compared with the performance of children who had attended the afternoon session. Then comparisons will be made between the performances of children taught by different teachers. There were three teachers in all in the pre-school, each of whom took a group of children in the morning and another group in the afternoon. (Children were randomly assigned to classes at the beginning of the programme.) On transferring to the junior school, the morning and afternoon groups of a teacher were combined into one class and remained with one teacher for the following three years. Thus, children who remained in the programme were taught by two teachers only — one in the pre-school, and a second one in the junior school. This, of course, did not apply to children who left the programme to attend other schools. In the analyses, the morning and afternoon children of a pre-school teacher were combined into one unit. The analyses which examine performance as related to session attended and to teachers should provide some information on the uniformity of implementation of the pre-school curriculum.

Performance at age eight will also be related to length of stay in the programme. Evidence from other studies on the relationship between length of programme and magnitude of effect is not entirely clear, though it does suggest a non-linear relationship with programmes of intermediate length proving to be the most effective. An examination of our data will permit us to look at effects over a relatively long period of time (five years), though it should be borne in mind that the last three years of the programme lacked the intensity of the first two years.

Differences, covering a variety of variables, were found between the performances of girls and boys in the programme. Girls performed better than boys in reading; their mean reading quotient on the Marino Word Recognition Test was 84.6 as against 74.0 for boys. There were also differences associated with personality and home background measures. Girls were rated more highly by teachers on a number of personality variables: on mood (i.e. they were perceived as being more cheerful and happy), on persistence (i.e. not readily bored or distracted) and on self-determination (i.e. in showing initiative). Girls' homes were rated as being characterized by a relatively high level of family activities, i.e. their families were more likely to engage in leisure activities together, to read books and periodicals and to make use of libraries and other resources. No difference was found between boys and girls in their level of intelligence as measured by the Stanford–Binet Scale.

Our finding on sex differences in reading ability, favouring girls, was not surprising in that such differences have frequently been reported for children of an age similar to the participants in the present investigation. Differences on a variety of personality measures have also been reported (*cf.* Maccoby, 1967). It appears that the girls in our study, in common with girls generally, were perceived as adapting better to the school situation than boys, a factor which in turn may not be unrelated to their higher level of reading attainment.

Attendance at a morning rather than at an afternoon session did not affect the performance of pupils. The teachers to whom children had been assigned, however, did affect later performance. Children associated with one set of teachers were significantly superior in intelligence (as measured by the Stanford–Binet Scale on which there was a difference of seven points and the Cattell test on which there was a nine point difference) to children taught by other teachers. The children of these teachers were also rated at eight years of age as being more competitive and less dependent than other pupils. Attainment, however, was not a discriminator between groups.

Finally, the relationship between performance at age eight and length of stay in the experimental programme was examined. In these analyses, children were categorized into three groups: those who left without completing the pre-school course (n: 17), those who completed the pre-school course but left without completing the junior school course in the school attached to the pre-school (n: 24), and those who completed the full programme — two years in the pre-school and three years in the junior school attached to the project (n: 49). Our findings indicate differences related to length of stay in programme but the relationship is not a simple or linear one. Neither are any of the differences related to intelligence or attainment. They relate only to non-cognitive variables, particularly home and personality ones. The children who completed the pre-school programme and left during the junior school period were characterized as possessing a high level of emotional control in situations of failure or frustration and came from homes which were rated as possessing a high degree of structure and routine. Children who left during the period of the pre-school were rated lowest of the three groups on these characteristics.

A number of points are relevant to a consideration of our data on length of stay in programme. Firstly, we were not in a position to investigate the effects of programme length, but only of length of stay in the programme since we did not have programmes that varied in length; neither did we have any control over how long a child stayed in the programme. The nature of the differences we observed relating to length of stay suggests that they are more likely a function of the children's homes than of their experience in the programme. The decision to leave the programme was made by parents. In some cases, this was because the family moved to live in another area. But in many cases, while continuing to live in the area of the pre-school, parents took the decision to send their children to a school outside the area. Traditionally, outside schools had higher prestige than the local schools in the eyes of parents and, since the schools served communities with families of mixed socioeconomic background, their levels of attainment were, not unexpectedly, higher than those of schools in the area of our investigation. Such factors may well have attracted parents with relatively high educational aspirations for their children to move them from the local school. Moving them, however, did not have the effect of raising their level of attainment beyond the level of children who stayed in the programme.

It should also be noted that our measure of length of stay in programme was rather crude. For example, we were not able to test the effects of length of stay in the pre-school itself, since not a sufficient number of children left during the pre-school period. Basically, what we investigated was the effect of staying more or less than two years in the total programme. Our inability to discriminate during the first two years may have removed the possibility of detecting effects of length of stay on cognitive development. A consideration of evidence from other studies (e.g. Karnes, 1973; Morrison, Watt, and Lee, 1974) and the fact that our own programme was more intensive during the first two years than during the succeeding three years suggest that length of stay was likely to be most critical during the pre-school period.

Conclusion

It was hypothesized in the present study that differences in the performances of the experimental and disadvantaged control groups would occur as a result of the pre-school intervention programme. Our analyses indicate clearly that such differences exist. The differences are primarily in terms of intelligence and home environment, only secondarily and marginally in terms of attainment, and hardly at all in terms of personality. Despite improvements in the performance of the children in the experimental group, their performance still falls far below that of children in non-disadvantaged areas. This is clear when we consider the amount of variance in discriminant space attributable to differences between groups. In the case of the comparison between the experimental and disadvantaged control groups, 57.6 per cent of the variance in discriminant space is attributable to differences between the groups. In other words, 57.6 per cent of the variability in the discriminant space is relevant to group differentiation. When the non-disadvantaged control group is added to the comparative analyses, the amount of variance attributable to differences between groups becomes larger (81.9 per cent). Thus, while there are differences between the experimental and the disadvantaged groups, the amount of variance explained increases considerably when an advantaged group is added.

When the experimental group is compared with the disadvantaged control group, the groups are most readily distinguishable in terms of intelligence, the experimental group being marked by a higher level of verbal intelligence. The addition of the non-disadvantaged control group to the analyses results in attainment becoming a more important group discriminator, the performance of the experimental group falling between that of the two control groups. Overall, however, the pre-school programme seems to have been more successful in raising the level of intelligence of participants than in raising their level of attainment.

A number of points are relevant to this conclusion. The main thrust of the pre-school programme was to raise the general level of intellectual functioning of the participants. The scores obtained by children on the Stanford—Binet test at the completion of the pre-school programme is indicative of considerable success in the attainment of its main objective (*cf.* Chapter V). However, it was assumed that a raising of the level of intelligence of the children would be accompanied by a raising of levels of attainment. This did not happen to any significant degree, or if it did happen initially, its effects had largely faded by the time the children were tested at eight years of age. We have already seen in Chapter V that when the children left the pre-school and at a time when they were starting the formal business of learning to read, a decline in their measured intelligence began to appear. This, as we have also seen, happened in other studies. It may be that influencing scholastic development is a more intransigent problem at the school level than at the pre-school level. Whether the problem is inherent in the nature of scholastic growth or a reflection on our skill as educators we do not know. However, it is clear that greater experimentation is possible in the pre-school, which is less inhibited by the conventions and constraints of the more established school. A more flexible approach to the education of children from disadvantaged backgrounds during their years of formal schooling seems clearly indicated. In any such approach, considerable attention needs to be given to the learning of reading — obviously still a major problem area for the children of the present investigation.

Whether comparisons involve only two groups or all three groups, home environment factors figure prominently as discriminators. The differences found between the homes of participants and of non-participants from similar backgrounds are of particular interest. It will be recalled that the involvement of children's parents was regarded as an important feature of the pre-school programme, and various efforts were made towards increasing this involvement. Homes were visited by teachers, and social workers maintained a liaison between the homes and the pre-school. Mothers frequently visited the school, both formally and informally, while fathers contributed to the maintenance of the school building. Can differences between the homes of experimental and non-experimental children be attributed to these efforts? In the absence of an alternative explanation, the answer would seem to be yes.

The diffuse nature of the effects of the pre-school programme, while it might be satisfactory from a practical point of view, creates problems in attempting to understand the working of the programme. On the one hand, we find effects on the children themselves in terms of their scholastic behaviour. We also find effects on their homes. An important question is how these effects may be related. Does the pre-school have its primary effect on the home and do the changed conditions in the home produce the observed effects on the children's behaviour? And if this is so, are there more effective and economical ways of influencing the home environment directly? Or is the pre-school institution an essential feature of the treatment, either in terms of its direct impact on the child or in terms of its impact on the home? Such questions cannot be answered on the basis of our investigation, but that they raise important issues is clear to anyone who is concerned with identifying the critical features of relatively successful programmes of early childhood education.

Our explorations of differences in performance of sub-groups within the experimental groups as well as underlining the complexity of the intervention procedure also serve to point to the need to explore more adequately in future investigations the critical features of programmes. They indicate that bright children benefited less from the programme than less bright ones, and that boys benefited less than girls. They also point to differences in implementation related to teachers; at the end of the programme one set of children differed from the other two sets in terms of measured intelligence and personality. Unfortunately, we cannot indicate how these differences might have arisen, since we have no data on the behaviour of teachers or children in the pre-school environment.

The data on length of stay in the programme serves to remind us that information collected in the school itself may not be sufficient in attempting to explain the development of participating children. Here we concluded that differences associated with length of stay were very likely to be less a result of the programme itself than a reflection of extra-school variables, in particular, the decisions of parents, which might have reflected their perceptions of the pre-school, their aspirations for the child's educational future, their perceptions of the quality of other schools, as well as factors, which might or might not have been within their control, such as the need to move to another area.

All of these findings point to the need for further investigations which will focus more on the workings of intervention programmes than on comparisons of group performances. While our results indicate that a pre-school programme can have limited effects, our efforts to increase programme effectiveness will, almost inevitably, continue to be limited until such time as we have more information about and a greater understanding of how programmes are implemented, about what aspects of them are most effective, and about how individual children and their families react to them.

Chapter VII

Parents' Reactions to the Pre-school

From the beginning of the project, it was considered important to ensure that the parents of children attending the pre-school would have positive attitudes toward the programme in operation in the school. Toward this end, a series of introductory meetings was held to inform the parents of the aims of the pre-school and also of some of the means it was proposed to take to attain these aims. Before the pre-school opened, each home was visited by a teacher and while the children were in the pre-school, homes were visited by a social worker to discuss the school progress of children. Throughout the duration of the project, parents were encouraged to visit the school whenever they wished; this provided the opportunity for them to see at first-hand the work of the pre-school. They were also able to discuss their children's progress with teachers.

Given this background of school—parent interaction, an assessment of parents' perceptions of the pre-school project was considered an important component of the overall evaluation of the programme. In this section, a survey of the responses, mainly attitudinal and affective, of a sample of mothers, whose children had attended the pre-school, is reported. A series of questions was designed to assess (i) the mothers' attitudes towards the pre-school; (ii) mothers' perceptions of the effects of the pre-school on their children; (iii) the extent to which behaviours of the mothers had changed as a result of pre-school contacts; and (iv) the mothers' attitudes towards the junior school, to which children could proceed for three years following their two years in the pre-school. There were 100 questions in the questionnaire; the responses to half the questions were open-ended.

Before describing the findings of the survey, we may note that interviews are subject to a number of well-documented limitations. How an interviewee responds to the specific formulation of a question is a function of her understanding of the question and of her experience with the issues involved at a particular point in time. Many events can intervene to change opinions over time. In addition, there is no guarantee that the respondents would react similarly to questions worded slightly differently.

The possible presence of a socially desirable response poses a further problem in the interpretation of subjective reports. Here, the response is influenced by what the respondent thinks the interviewer wants to hear. To counteract this tendency in the present study, negative responses were listed prior to positive ones in closed-ended items of the questionnaire. Furthermore, open-ended responses were used to make better estimates of the respondent's true intentions. Another limitation of survey data is that statistical summaries of responses to various questions can be misleading if they are considered in terms of a majority or plurality. 'Only thirty per cent' may be a considerable number of people. Besides, the characteristics of this group might be such that their opinions should receive more weight than the seventy per cent answering the same item in a different way.

In interpreting survey results, it should be remembered that all sample surveys are subject to sampling error. Sampling error indicates the extent to which the results may differ from what would have been obtained if the total population (in our case 90 mothers) had been interviewed. The size of such sampling error depends largely on the number of interviews. Since the sample size in the present study was quite small (n: 25) no significance should be attached to small differences in the numbers of respondents selecting various options to the same question.

Mothers of 25 of the children who had attended the pre-school and were still living in the Dublin area (n: 86) were randomly selected for interview. Two of these mothers could not be contacted for interview and were replaced by two others. All but three of the children of mothers in the sample stayed in the pre-school for the full two-year period. One family had moved out of the area; for another mother, the time of the pre-school was inconvenient, and the remaining mother removed her child because he had been 'hit by another child'.

The mean number of children in the families of each of the mothers sampled was 6.2 (SD: 3.1). However, some households had as many as eleven children while others had as few as two. Boys and girls were not equally represented in the sample; ten of the mothers had boys in the pre-school; the remaining fifteen were mothers of girls. A sizeable percentage (40 per cent) of the respondents had moved from the area in which the pre-school was located to other areas in the city. These moves were prompted by considerations of improved space and facilities, health, safety and proximity to relatives. Slightly over half the mothers had themselves left school at the end of primary schooling (sixth class). The remaining mothers were equally divided between those who did not go farther than fifth class and those who had completed one year beyond sixth class, either in a vocational school or in seventh class in a primary school (equivalent to a first year post-primary class). Approximately half of the mothers were aged between 31 and 40; one-third were between 41 and 50 and the remaining ones were less than 30 years of age.

Interviews were conducted in the homes of the mothers over a period of ten days after the children had been tested in the final evaluation of the project. Thus the children to whom the interviews refer were aged eight years at the time of the interview. Interviews were carried out by a qualified teacher who had previous survey experience. The interviewer had no prior contact with the pre-school or the junior school and was not known by any of the pre-school staff or parents.

Closed-ended responses in the interview questionnaire were coded. The responses given by mothers to open-ended items were used as the basis for establishing categories for these items. The open-ended items were then coded according to these categories. Frequency-counts and percentages were tabulated for the responses to each item in the questionnaire.

A series of χ^2 analyses of mothers' responses by education of the mother, family size, location, age of mother and sex of child in the project did not reveal any significant relationships between these variables and issues concerning the pre-school or the junior school.

Mothers' attitudes towards the pre-school

A series of questions was included in the questionnaire to assess the mothers' attitudes towards various aspects of the pre-school. The questions ranged from specific items dealing with aspects of the programme such as the evaluation of teachers and of the curriculum to general questions about overall satisfaction with the pre-school.

Mothers' reasons for sending children to the pre-school were varied. Eight mentioned the quality or special function of the pre-school, five mentioned peer group companionship and three saw it as a preparation for future education. The purposes of the pre-school as perceived by parents are presented in Table 7.1. Here it will be seen that more than half the parents saw the pre-school primarily in educational terms.

When the pre-school was opened, a series of meetings had been held to introduce parents to the pre-school. The vast majority of the mothers interviewed had attended at least one such meeting; one parent could not remember if she had attended a meeting or not. All who attended were positive in their evaluation of the meetings, rating them either as very helpful or fairly helpful. Several reasons were given by the mothers for their positive evaluations. They saw the meetings as providing information on the methods and content of instruction, as providing an insight and advice relating to one's own child, as serving a general educational function for the parents themselves, and as providing the opportunity for parents to get to know teachers and other parents. When asked if they could remember anything specific that was said at these meetings, several mothers proceeded to quote statements made by members of the pre-school staff. 'A child's first teacher is his parent said the social worker,' recalled one parent. Another enthusiastically remembered that 'Mr Holland (director of the pre-school) once said parents are always saying to their children that they have not got the time to listen to their problems and he said "let's face it, we can make time to listen to the children".'

Table 7.1: Purpose of the pre-school as perceived by parents

Category	N
Preparation for regular school / future education	3
Positive function of education	8
Offset negative environmental factors	2
Care-taking function	5
Disciplinary function	2
Teaching of social skills and recreational function	3
Explorational	1
Don't know / uncertain	1

All the mothers had met their children's pre-school teachers. When asked to evaluate the teacher's work, the mothers stated that the teachers were doing a good job. Their positive attitude towards the work of the teacher was based on her overall interest (about a quarter), a noticeable change in the child's 'behaviour' (a quarter), the happiness of the child in class (a fifth), the child's academic advancement (a fifth) and finally the teaching methods (less than a tenth). Given the positive evaluation of the teachers' work by the parents, it was not surprising to find that all but one of the mothers found the teachers very interested in their children. There was somewhat less agreement among mothers on the question of discipline in the pre-school. A majority, two out of three mothers, felt that the teachers were strict enough. However, a quarter found the teachers too easy. In answer to the question, 'Is there anything that should have been taught in the pre-school that was not taught when your child was there?', almost nine out of ten mothers found the curriculum adequate. Only one mother saw an inadequacy — she wished that her daughter had been taught 'how to sit properly on a chair.' Two parents were not sure if anything had been lacking.

Clearly the picture emerges of mothers satisfied with what was being taught in the school. But what did the respondents think their children were learning? Mothers were asked if they could remember any specific things that their children learned in the pre-school. A summary of responses to this question is outlined in Table 7.2. The category of activity mentioned most often was coded. For example, if the respondent listed reading, writing and counting, the responses were classified scholastic. Where all categories were given the same degree of emphasis, the first option was coded. Table 7.2 clearly indicates that mothers had different perceptions of the type of 'curriculum' pursued within the pre-school. The largest number of mothers cited non-scholastic skills as being characteristic of what their children had learned. One mother in five selected scholastic skills, such as reading, writing and counting. Personal cleanliness and proper behaviour were mentioned by a smaller number. One mother didn't see the child as learning anything. Most interesting perhaps is the fact that a fifth of the respondents who claimed to be satisfied with the curriculum couldn't remember anything the child had learned in the pre-school.

A large majority of mothers (20) indicated that much time was spent playing in the classrooms. Quite frequently parents do not consider play in the context of their children's growth and development. In the present survey however, it was found that all but three of the mothers considered play as either 'important' or 'fairly important'. A number of reasons were given for the high value placed on play. In order of frequency of response, these were: play provides a means of teaching the child through using and doing; the play was enjoyed by children and it helped them mix with other children; it helped the child to become interested in objects around him or her; and finally results of play were seen by the mothers in the things the child could do at home.

A number of ancillary services were provided in the pre-school and parents' reactions to these were elicited. Weekly visits were made to the school by a physician. Slightly more than four out of five found these visits helpful. Another ancillary service was provided by the social worker. Twenty-one of the 25 mothers remembered having had a visit from a social worker while their children were in the pre-school. Approximately two out of five rated her visits as being very helpful

Table 7.2: Specific things learned in the pre-school as perceived by parents

Category	N
Scholastic skills such as reading, writing, counting	5
Non-scholastic skills such as drawing, water-play etc.	11
Personal cleanliness / behaviour	3
Doesn't see child as learning anything	1
Can't remember	5

while a similar figure rated her visit 'a little helpful'. One of the most frequently mentioned reasons why mothers were positive in their evaluation of the social worker was adequately expressed by the mother who observed 'If you had any problem, you felt she would have done her best.'

In general, the mothers expressed satisfaction with the pre-school, in particular, and with the idea of pre-schooling in general. As far as the particular pre-school was concerned, three-quarters of the mothers indicated that there were no changes that they wished to see made in it. A minority (four mothers) mentioned such changes as eliminating water-play, removing mothers from classrooms or extending the hours of the school day. It is interesting to note that in answer to the question, 'would you have liked your child to stay at the pre-school for a longer time during the day?', almost three-fourths of the mothers answered in the affirmative. Of those who favoured a longer day, over two-thirds sought an extension of from one to two hours, while almost a third would have lengthened the day by as much as 2½ to three hours.

In keeping with the positive attitudes already expressed by mothers towards various aspects of the pre-school with which they had experience, it is not surprising that all mothers agreed that there should be more pre-school provision around the country. Table 7.3 summarizes the reasons for this given by the respondents. Close to one in five mothers felt that the pre-school helped the child prepare for later schooling. An equal number felt that the pre-school was good for parents too. One commented: 'A pre-school gives a lot of mothers a break.' A fifth were not specific and simply felt that the pre-school was a good place to go at that age. An equal number expressed a vague general positive attitude towards the pre-school. Two mothers mentioned facilities such as 'there is good heating there' and 'they get dinner and milk'.

Table 7.3: Reasons for more pre-schools as perceived by parents

Category	N
Good place to go at that age	5
Gives children a better 'chance' of coping with school	6
Good for parents	6
Facilities good	2
Positive attitude (general)	5
Don't know	1

Another indication of positive attitude toward the pre-school is the mother's view of how attending the pre-school had helped her child later in the junior school. Two-thirds of mothers felt that the child was helped 'a great deal' in junior school by the pre-school experience. Three mothers indicated that it had helped the child a little, while four had found the pre-school of no help. Those mothers who felt that the pre-school had a positive influence on junior school performance had difficulty articulating specific reasons for this view. As one mother noted, 'It (the pre-school) did help her, but I couldn't say more about how it did.'

An indirect measure of mothers' attitude toward the pre-school was obtained through the question: 'If a friend asked you whether she should send her three-year-old child to the pre-school would you say: keep the child at home; send the child to a pre-school other than the one attended by your child; send the child to pre-school attended by your child, or you're not sure, you don't know.' All but three parents indicated that they would recommend that the friend sent the child to the pre-school attended by their child. Only one indicated that the child should be sent to a different pre-school, while two were not sure of what advice they would offer. It should be stressed that no mother recommended that the child be kept at home.

When asked why they would recommend the pre-school attended by their own child, a majority of mothers (16) cited favourable experiences with their own children as the best reasons. According to one mother, 'They (the children) gain a lot and lose nothing.' A number mentioned the qualities of the school itself (safe place) as a reason for recommendation. Only one mother stated that the pre-school was 'good for parents if they want to leave children for a while.' Interestingly enough, mothers' recommendations of the pre-school were based upon perceived beneficial results for the child rather than on the 'handiness' of the school for the friend.

The findings we have been considering indicate clearly a very positive attitude towards the pre-school on the part of mothers. One question in the interview sought to assess fathers' attitudes towards the pre-school. Mothers' responses to this question indicated that their husbands, without exception, also had positive attitudes. Since the question was not directed to the fathers themselves, however, there is no reason to assume that all of them would have been as positive as the one father who was present at the interview and commented: 'I was born and reared here and think it's (pre-school) the greatest thing ever happened here.'

Mothers' perceptions of effects of pre-school on child

While mothers' attitudes towards the pre-school may have been influenced by their experiences at the introductory meetings and by their frequent visits to the school and the observations of peers, it is unlikely that any of these factors influenced them to the same extent as their perceptions of the effects of the pre-school on their own children.

First of all, there was the question of the children's own satisfaction with the pre-school. Mothers' responses to the question 'Did your child like the pre-school?' leave little doubt that the children had favourable attitudes towards pre-school. All but two claimed that their children 'liked it a lot,' whereas the remaining two claimed they 'liked it a little.' Further questioning of the mothers revealed a variety of reasons why the children liked the pre-school (Table 7.4). Mothers' responses indicated that the friendliness of the teachers, the general atmosphere of the school and the activities that were available in the school were the most important factors. A separate question asked whether the child liked his / her teacher. All but one indicated that their children liked her a lot.

Mothers were also asked if their children developed any particular interests while they were going to the pre-school. Almost half the mothers noticed that their children had developed some scholastic interests, such as in reading, while a similar number observed that their children had developed interests in somewhat less traditionally scholastic areas such as in drawing. The remaining mothers commented that their children's primary interests were outside the school (e.g. in football, cars and soldiers). Those parents who observed an increased interest in reading may have been influenced by the frequency with which the children brought home books from the school library. According to the parents, 16 pupils brought books home at least a few times a week, while five brought books home a few times a month. Four children never brought home books from the school library.

Table 7.4: Reasons why children liked pre-school as perceived by parents

Category	N
Activities in the pre-school	5
Friendly teachers	10
General environment and atmosphere of freedom	6
Companionship of other children	2
Not sure	2

Had the companionship of the pre-school helped children to get on better with their peers? Seven of the mothers said that their children had no problem getting on with other children before they went to the pre-school; sixteen however, claimed that the pre-school had been of some help to their children in peer-group relationships. Mothers had great difficulty in identifying specific aspects of the pre-school setting that contributed to this improvement. They simply claimed that the particular environment of the pre-school provided the opportunity of 'learning to mix.'

Mothers were asked also to comment on whether the pre-school experience had helped their children to get on better with their parents. While half the mothers did not perceive their children as having had any problem in this area, most of the remaining half noted that the pre-school experience had indeed helped this relationship. The improvement in the relationship was most often attributed to the increased verbal facility of the child. Mothers mentioned that children had learned new words which made it easier for them to communicate. Furthermore, the respondents noted that the experiences in the pre-school provided topics for conversation.

Did mothers notice any ways in which the pre-school child was different from his older siblings who had not attended the pre-school? Eight mothers saw no difference and three noted a difference (scholastically or in general behaviour) in favour of older siblings. Five mothers however, noticed greater alertness among the pre-schoolers. One mother commented 'She picked up things quicker. The pre-school made it easier for me to explain things like clocks and shapes to her.' The remaining mothers noticed improvements in general behaviour.

Effects of pre-school on mothers' behaviour

It has been argued that parents of working class and disadvantaged children do not regard themselves as educators of their children to the same extent as middle class parents. It was hoped that contacts with the pre-school would bring about changes in parental behaviour that would positively affect the intellectual and personality development of their children. A number of questions were included in the questionnaire to ascertain whether any such changes did, in fact, take place during the course of the five-year programme.

At the outset it should be noted that most mothers (22) in the sample had older children who had not attended the pre-school. Almost half these mothers stated that they spent more time with the pre-school child at home than they had spent with their other children when they were younger. These mothers indicated that their pre-school children talked more or demanded more attention than their older children had. Typical remarks of this group of respondents included the following: 'He would show you his work and ask you to check it for him'; 'he used to talk a lot about school and what he did and you would have to listen'; 'I would sit down a lot more with him and his books and get him to learn, — the others did not bring home books.'

We noted above that more than four out of five pre-school children had brought books home from the school library on a regular basis. Almost half of the mothers of these children read to them daily while another one-third read to them a few times a week. Two mothers confined their reading to a few times a month.

A series of questions was included in the questionnaire to determine if mothers had learned (i.e. put into practice on the basis of their experience with the pre-school) anything about discipline, teaching methods, toy selection, or verbal communication with their children. Whenever a positive response was given for any of these dimensions, the respondent was asked to elaborate on the 'new' method or procedure that she had learned.

With regard to discipline, just over half the mothers claimed that they had not learned anything new about it. One in five mothers indicated that they had learned something new, while the remaining mothers were not sure if they had learned anything new. Among those who had indicated a change in attitude towards discipline, frequent mention was made of the need for talking to children rather than resorting to physical punishment as the only form of discipline. As one parent observed, 'They taught me how to talk him out of something rather than giving him a belt.'

In general, mothers in the sample were positive in their evaluation of the play opportunities afforded the pre-school children. As far as playing at home was concerned, half of the mothers indicated that they would prefer to buy 'education'-type toys for their children — 'something that made their minds work.' One-third of the mothers indicated that they would buy specific items that had been recommended such as books, bricks and paints. A minority (four) stated that they would give no special thought to buying a toy or would buy something the child wanted.

A quarter of the mothers claimed that the pre-school had shown them ways of talking to their children that they did not know before. These new approaches included such things as 'answering questions instead of putting the child off,' and 'not speaking to them like they were babies.' Approximately half of all mothers acknowledged that the pre-school had shown them ways of teaching their children that they had not known before. Specific instructional techniques such as the use of word-cards and word attack skills were mentioned as ways of helping children with reading and spelling. A lesser number of respondents felt that reading to their children and answering their questions were ways of helping that they had not considered before. In general, mothers were regular visitors in the pre-school classrooms of their children. Two out of five mothers visited the classroom daily; over a fifth did so a few times a week while one-fifth visited a few times a month.

When mothers with older children were asked how the amount of time they spent in the pre-school compared with the amount they spent in the schools of their older children, all but one said that they spent more time in the pre-school. They felt they were not allowed in the schools of their older children. One parent noted, 'You don't go in a national school.' Another observed 'Teachers don't want you in there.' By contrast, in the pre-school, 'You were invited all the time and they (teachers) approved of parents coming in and seeing for themselves.'

Mothers' attitudes towards junior school

After spending two years in the pre-school programme, it was expected that the children would transfer to the junior school which was adjacent to the pre-school. So far, we have been considering mothers' attitudes to the pre-school. In this section, we shall focus on mothers' attitudes towards the junior school.

Twenty-one of the children transferred to the local junior school after completing pre-school. A number of reasons were given by mothers for sending their children to this school. Approximately half acknowledged that the junior school was part of the project and, as such, was a continuation of the pre-school. A quarter of respondents felt that the changeover 'just happened; they (the children) were "passed over".' The response of a few mothers suggested that their children were sent to the junior school because all the other children were going, while another small group claimed to have sent their children there because of its location and quality. These comments seem to indicate a certain degree of passiveness on the part of the parents. In many instances it appears that no active choice was made to send their children to the local junior school; rather it seemed a matter of letting events take their own course. This latter conclusion is supported by the evidence that four out of five parents, in response to the question whether they had thought about sending the child to any other school, indicated that they had given it no thought. It may also be possible that mothers may not have thought about another school because they consciously wanted their children to continue in the project for five years.

The reasons volunteered by the four mothers whose children did not go to the junior school varied. Two families had moved out of the area. One mother did not send her child because she felt that the children in the school were a bad influence. The fourth mother sought a longer school day for her child. Of the two mothers who had moved out of the locality, one indicated that she would have sent her child to the junior school if she had not moved, as her child had done well in the pre-school. The other, however, would not have sent her child because of the bad influence she perceived other children as having on him.

At the time of the administration of the present questionnaire, the majority of children had finished the junior school. Mothers were asked if they had to make the choice of a junior school again, would they still send their children to the same school. Almost three-quarters said they would. However, the remainder (a sizeable minority) indicated that they would choose another school, giving as their reason a desire for more discipline and more teacher interest in their children. A number also felt that their children's friends had had a bad influence, both socially and intellectually, on their children. Transfer from the junior school before completing the three-year course might also be an indication of dissatisfaction. Three children transferred from the junior school because they were leaving the locality; two others left because of problems of discipline while the mothers of the remaining two claimed that their children were unhappy in the school.

Mothers were asked to compare the local junior school with other junior schools in neighbouring areas. While just over half of those interviewed felt that the local school was as good as or better than the neighbouring junior schools, a sizeable minority (a third) were not sure how the school compared with other schools in the area. At the other extreme, two parents claimed that the local school was worse than neighbouring junior schools.

An indirect measure of the mothers' attitude to the junior school was obtained by asking them to compare the present junior school with the junior school as it was five years earlier. Nine mothers said that the present school was better. A similar number were not sure, while three mothers indicated that the present school was about as good as the older school. It was significant that none of the parents, all of whom would have been familiar with the previous school, considered the older school better than the present one. Further questioning revealed that satisfaction with school discipline was the main reason for the positive evaluation of the junior school. A separate question on school discipline revealed that a majority (15) of mothers considered it 'just strict enough.' When pressed for reasons for this opinion, these mothers indicated that the teachers understood the children and controlled them. In addition, mothers commented that their children didn't complain about the school.

Nine out of ten mothers had met the child's junior school teacher. When asked to evaluate the teachers' work, three-quarters of the mothers indicated that the teachers had done a good job of teaching their children. The remaining evaluation of teaching ranged from fair (one mother) to poor (two mothers) to not sure (two mothers). Of those mothers who felt that the teachers did a good job in teaching their children, seven out of ten cited the past or present scholastic achievement of their children as evidence of good teaching. As in the case of the pre-school, an overwhelming majority of mothers (19 out of 21) stated that the teachers were interested in their children. A separate question revealed that four out of five children liked the junior school teachers.

Approximately six out of ten mothers thought that their children received 'just enough' homework. However, a sizeable minority, almost three out of ten, felt that there was too little homework. The remaining mothers indicated that they had no opinions on the issue.

The positive evaluation of the junior school was supported by mothers' answers to the questions: 'If there was anything about junior school that you would change what would it be?' In general, parents were satisfied with the *status quo* and did not desire any change. Of the minority who requested change, more discipline was the factor most often cited. A further small number of mothers mentioned that they would have welcomed more contact with the junior school teachers.

Conclusion

In this survey of mothers' reactions to the pre-school, a variety of reasons was offered for sending children to the pre-school. The explanatory meetings about the role of the school at the beginning of the project were considered very helpful. A high level of satisfaction with the pre-school in general was reported. Teachers were perceived as having done 'a good job' and as being interested in the children, and the curriculum was also considered satisfactory. Further questioning on the curriculum revealed that most of the mothers recalled children learning non-scholastic, as opposed to scholastic, skills. The ancillary services of both doctor and social worker were highly valued. Among perceived effects of the pre-school were the positive attitudes of the children themselves toward the pre-school. Mothers also felt that the children had developed scholastic and school-related interests. A majority considered that the pre-school experiment had helped their children by the time they got to junior school. More than half of the children brought books home from the library on a regular basis. A minority of the respondents also observed positive differences between their pre-school children and older siblings who had not had pre-school experience.

In addition to noticing change in their children's attitudes, mothers also observed a number of behavioural changes in their own interactions with their children. As a result of their direct experience with the pre-school, mothers observed an increase in the extent of verbal communication between themselves and their children. A small number also reported a change (away from corporal punishment) in attitudes toward discipline. A good proportion read to their children every day. A minority of respondents also indicated that they had learned new ways of teaching their children. Lastly, they visited the classrooms of their pre-school children on a regular basis. Almost all spent more time in the pre-school classroom than in the classrooms of their older children. This latter difference was attributed to the greater degree of encouragement received from the teachers in the pre-school to visit the classroom.

A large minority of the pre-school pupils transferred to the junior school at the end of the pre-school period. Most mothers seem to have accepted the local junior school as a natural progression from the pre-school. Three years later, two-thirds of the children were still enrolled in the junior school. The remaining one-third had either moved out of the area or had left due to problems of discipline or general unhappiness with the school.

In general, the survey reveals the high impact of the pre-school on the homes of the children. Parents were more actively involved in the education of their children — both at home and in school — following their experience of the pre-school than they had been beforehand. Furthermore, the general reaction of the parents to this situation was one of satisfaction and approval.

Chapter VIII

Conclusions

In this report, the evaluation of the impact of a project designed to assist the educational development of children in an inner city disadvantaged area has been described. The project took the form of a special educational programme for children aged between three and eight years. The main thrust of the project was at the pre-school level (attended by three- to five-year-old children) for which a special curriculum was developed; less structured attempts were also made in the junior school (attended by five- to eight-year-old children) to adapt the primary school curriculum to the needs of the children.

The pre-school programme had two major components — a specially developed curriculum and a programme for parental involvement. The curriculum was planned primarily with cognitive—scholastic objectives in mind. In general terms, the objective of the curriculum was to develop skills that would facilitate the children's adaptation to the work of the primary school. It was hoped that the programme would have the effect of improving the rate of cognitive and scholastic development of participating children. Major foci of the curriculum were the development of skills of perceptual discrimination, the extension of the child's knowledge of the world, particularly of his immediate environment, the development of skills in the organization of knowledge and the development of language skills. Personality, social and motivational development also received attention, though less than cognitive development, in curriculum formulations. Structure was an important element of the cognitive components of the curriculum. Insofar as possible, teachers specified objectives and then planned activities that were designed to work towards the attainment of these objectives; specific times were allocated for the activities.

The programme for parental involvement had a number of aspects. Teachers visited the homes of the children and so had the opportunity of observing each individual child's home circumstances. Mothers, on the other hand, were encouraged to visit the school so that they could learn something of its objectives and the means it was taking to achieve those objectives. Parent–teacher meetings were also a feature of the programme and attempts were made to involve fathers as well as mothers in the education of their children. Finally, social workers maintained links between the homes of the children and the schools.

Information collected at the beginning of the project indicated that children living in the area which was the focus of investigation were in need of special assistance in their schooling. In the absence of intervention, one could expect a high degree of school failure. The extent of this failure was evidenced in the test results obtained at the beginning of the project for a sample of eight-year-olds living in the area. On tests of perception, verbal ability and attainment, these children scored well below the mean of a group of children living in non-disadvantaged areas in the same city. Scores on measures of the home environment, such as the achievement press of the home, the quality of language used and the opportunities for the pursuit of intellectual activities, were also below the mean obtained by the non-disadvantaged sample.

The performance of the three-year-olds in the area on tests of verbal ability and other cognitive measures was found to be below the published norms for these measures. Data for control group children in other areas of the same city were not available, as had been in the case of the eight-year-olds; nevertheless, one can assume that performance relative to such a group would also have been depressed. However, the degree of retardation in the three-year-old group did not seem as great as in the case of the eight-year-olds. It would appear that as far as scholastic behaviour is concerned, the longer children live in a disadvantaged area, the more unlike children living in more 'normal' environments they become.

Main findings

During the five years of the project, the intellectual development of children (n: 90) was monitored. Mean scores of the group on the Stanford–Binet Intelligence Scale showed an increase from a mean IQ of 92.99 (SD: 13.10) on entry to one of 99.44 (SD: 13.96) on the completion of two years of pre-schooling. This was followed by a decline during the three years in the junior school; mean IQ at the end of the project, when the children were eight years of age, was 90.91 (SD: 11.16). While the final score of the group is about the same as the score when they started, these figures should be seen in the context of an expected decline from the position at initial testing if no intervention programme had been available. The mean IQ of eight-year-olds in the area before the project began was found to be 84.71 (SD: 16.49).

A comparison of the performances of participating children on the Preschool Inventory at ages three and five years provides evidence of improvement in their achievement 'in areas regarded as necessary for success in school' (Caldwell, 1967). Improvement was noted particularly in the ability of the children to respond to verbal communication, in their vocabulary and in their knowledge of numerical concepts. At the age of six, the performance of the group seemed satisfactory in terms of American norms on a range of pre-reading skills (visual and auditory discrimination though not visual-motor coordination).

A number of other points may be made about the development of children during the course of the project. Firstly, we considered the nature of the intellectual development of the children as reflected in their performance on various sets of items of the Stanford—Binet Scale. Our analyses suggest that the group, while performing at a somewhat lower level than the standardization sample (with the exception of their performance at age five which was equal to that of the standardization sample), do not differ from them in their patterns of response to items on the test. Thus, insofar as different aspects of intellectual functioning are measured by the Stanford—Binet test, the experimental group does not differ qualitatively from the standardization sample in the nature of its intellectual functioning. This does not mean that a wider range of tests would not have revealed the existence of differences.

Another finding that emerges from our analyses relates to the heterogeneity of the group of children in the study. Children from disadvantaged areas are not uniformly backward. On all the tests administered, a wide variation in performance was found. The lowest IQ score recorded at age three, for example, was 59; the highest was 125. At age eight, the lowest IQ was 68 and the highest 128. On the English reading test at age eight, some children received the lowest possible score, which in effect means they failed to pronounce correctly even one word on the test. On the other hand, one child had a reading age of 13.1 years. There is thus a vast range of differences in the performance of the children on measures of scholastic aptitude and attainment. Obviously, it is incorrect to treat all children from disadvantaged areas as if they formed a homogeneous group.

A further general point about our findings also relates to the variance of the scores of the children. While the range of differences in the experimental group was large, the variance in intelligence test scores actually decreased as the children grew older and was also smaller than the variance of children who had been living in the area prior to the introduction of the intervention project. A closer examination of this phenomenon revealed that the decrease in variance was to some extent the result of a loss in the number of high scores among the group after they had left the pre-school. This suggests that brighter children benefitted less from the programme than less able ones, a view that is substantiated by a consideration of the regression of scores at age eight on scores at age five, in which there was some evidence of a regression discontinuity, lower scorers tending to gain more over the three-year period than higher scorers. To achieve optimal development, it may be that more able children require a range of experiences that were not available in the programme, particularly during their period in the junior school.

Girls in the project did better than boys — not in intelligence, but in their reading attainment. They were also rated more highly on a number of personality measures — on mood, persistence and self-determination. These results provide support for findings, which have been frequently reported in the literature, relating to sex differences in scholastic attainment and personality, for samples of children from a variety of backgrounds (Maccoby, 1967).

In evaluating the global effectiveness of the intervention programme, comparisons were made on a number of variables between the performance of the children who had participated in the programme (when they reached the age of eight years) and the performance of eight-year-old children who had been living in the area prior to the introduction of the intervention programme. The results of statistical analysis indicated that the two groups differed significantly from each other. In a discriminant function analysis, the function that most clearly differentiated the groups was heavily weighted by intelligence; the next heaviest weights were attached to home environment measures. A child who had been through the experimental programme was likely to score higher on the Stanford—Binet Intelligence test than a child who had not, while his home was likely to be rated more highly in terms of the general quality of its language, in opportunities for language development, in the availability of guidance on matters relating to school work and in the availability and use of materials and facilities related to school learning.

The performance of the children who had participated in the programme was compared not only with that of a control group from the same background but also with the performance of a group of children of similar age from non-disadvantaged backgrounds. In analyses, the three groups were clearly separated. The major discriminator between the groups had a large attainment component; a second function that discriminated between the groups had a large intelligence component along a verbal—non-verbal continuum, with some weighting from home factors. In terms of the two functions, the group from non-disadvantaged backgrounds was high on attainment and intermediate on the verbal—non-verbal intelligence function. The group from the disadvantaged area who had not participated in the experimental programme was low on attainment and fell towards the non-verbal end of the intelligence function. The group that had participated in the programme was relatively low on attainment (though not as low as the disadvantaged group who had not participated in the programme) and fell towards the verbal end of the intelligence function.

An important aspect of these findings is the difference which was found between the homes of the experimental group and the homes of children from the same area who had not participated in the programme. Personality variables did not discriminate between participants and non-participants from disadvantaged backgrounds. The two groups from the disadvantaged background, however, did differ in personality from children living in non-disadvantaged backgrounds. Of all the areas investigated, it was on the personalities of the children that the programme seemed to have had least impact.

Finally, in evaluating the pre-school programme, the reactions of parents were obtained. There were two aspects to this — one, their attitude toward the programme, and the other, their perception of the effects of the programme on their children. In a survey carried out in a sample of parents of children who had participated in the project, a high level of satisfaction with the pre-school was reported. For a variety of reasons, parents liked the idea of the pre-school and were happy with the way in which it was run. Furthermore, the parents saw the children as having positive attitudes towards the pre-school. In terms of the perceived effects of the programme, mothers felt that the children had developed scholastic and school-related interests. They also reported an increase in the extent of verbal communication between themselves and their children. For example, a number reported a change away from corporal punishment in attitudes toward discipline, a good proportion read to their children every day, and a small number indicated that they had learned new ways of teaching their children. Here again, we see evidence of the effectiveness of the programme in the homes of the children.

Limitations of the evaluation procedure

To examine possible limitations of our evaluation procedures, we will return to a consideration of the basic questions we sought to answer in this evaluation (*cf.* Chapter IV). The first question was, have the programme objectives been achieved? If we accept that the main objective of our study was to raise the level of performance of the participants on tests of general cognitive functioning and attainment, then the answer will be both yes and no. No specific level of performance was specified in the objectives. If a level of performance higher than that of children from a similar background who had not participated in the programme is accepted as the criterion of success, then the programme largely achieved its objectives. If however, the criterion of success is performance at the level of non-disadvantaged children, then we must distinguish between performance at the end of the pre-school and performance at the end of the junior school. At the end of the pre-school, as we have seen, the developmental progress of the children in the cognitive and attainment areas compared well with that of children from non-disadvantaged backgrounds. Initial improvement was, however, followed by a decline in the cognitive and scholastic performance of the participating children and, by the end of the junior school period, while still performing better than non-participants from disadvantaged backgrounds, their performance relative to non-disadvantaged children had deteriorated.

The second basic question relating to our evaluation asks if programme services accounted for the achievement of objectives. In attempting to answer this question, it is necessary to consider the validity of our experimental design, since inferences concerning programme effectiveness are a function of design validity (Campbell and Stanley, 1963). Problems relating to validity are partly technical and partly the result of the 'real world' context in which a programme such as the one we are considering was carried out (Little and Smith, 1971). A consideration of some of the threats to the validity of the design of the present evaluation will be of assistance in attempting to determine if the differences we observed can be attributed to our experimental treatment. A number of factors are relevant to a consideration of the *internal* validity of a design. If not controlled, these might produce effects which could be confounded with the effects of the experimental treatment, or, on the other hand, could lead to conclusions about the non-effectiveness of a treatment which would not be warranted. A further set of factors relates to the *external* validity of a design, which pertains to the question of generalizability, i.e. the populations and settings to which the effects can be generalized.

In considering internal validity, the question of the sensitivity of the criterion measures arises. This in turn relates to the objectives of the programme. A clear statement of objectives, while it may always be desirable, particularly from the evaluator's point of view, is not always possible. One has to accept that objectives often cannot be precisely defined and are resistant to precise measurement (Halsey, 1972). In the present study, given its general aims, we have argued the appropriateness of a test of general intellectual functioning as the criterion measure. Measures of school attainment were also included. The appropriateness of conventional standardized tests in the evaluation of curricula and school programmes is now a matter of controversy, which has yet to be resolved, although recent evidence indicates that in some circumstances more sensitive measures are available (Madaus, Kellaghan and Rakow, 1975). There has, however, been little by way of development of such measures for use with pre-school children. The Preschool Inventory goes some way towards providing an instrument that is sensitive to the goals of pre-school education with a cognitive bias, and, as we saw, an analysis of children's performance on the test can provide some specific indications of changes in children's knowledge during the pre-school years. While arguing that the measures which we used seemed adequate in the context of the instruments that were available when our study was designed, it is not our intention to deny the need for the development of more appropriate measures for use in future studies. For such development, investigators may have to look beyond traditional test development procedures.

Also relevant to a consideration of criterion measures is the question of repeated testing which relates to the effects of taking a test upon the scores of a later testing. The members of the experimental group, it will be recalled, were exposed to testing on numerous occasions. Extensive testing was carried out at the beginning of the pre-school programme when the children were three years of age and the children were tested on the Stanford–Binet Scale each year up to the age of eight. By contrast, the testing of members of the control group at eight years of age was this group's first experience of psychological testing. We considered this issue in some detail when considering results on the Stanford–Binet testings and our conclusion was that the performance of the group was not likely to have been significantly influenced by previous exposures to the test. Besides, many of the tests which the experimental group took in the final evaluation had not been taken before by the group.

More subtly, it could be argued that, irrespective of familiarity with the content of specific tests, the greater familiarity of the experimental group with the test situation could have worked to their advantage. Because of such factors as motivation and a greater understanding of the implicit rules of the test situation (e.g. being required to answer questions simply for the sake of answering), the experimental group might have performed better than the control group (Glick, 1968). Using Philip Vernon's (1961) extension of Hebb's (1949) terminology, this would imply that the experimental group would appear better on Intelligence C ('test performance') though the difference between them and the control group on Intelligence B ('developmental intelligence' or the cognitive abilities built up in infancy and childhood) might be negligible. It does not seem at all improbable that the experimental group adapted to testing better than the control group. However, a more likely explanation of this adaptation is probably to be found in their greater experience of school and of the constraints of schooling which one might have expected to transfer to a formal test situation. If such a transfer did, in fact, take place, it can hardly be regarded as artifactual or inconsequential. It is also unlikely that it referred only to test-taking skills and did not affect the underlying trait being tested.

Another reason for the differences in test performance between the experimental and control groups might be sought in the different experiences of the groups, apart altogether from the experience of the intervention programme by one of the groups. While this is a problem in any quasi-experiment — one can never be sure that the experience or history of experimental and control groups has been alike in all ways except for the manipulated treatment — the design of the present study created particular problems. It will be recalled that the control group was tested *before* the intervention programme began; thus, there was a five-year lag between the testing of the control and experimental groups. If conditions generally had changed during that five years — for example, if housing and home conditions had improved remarkably, if general levels of attainment had risen through the school system — then differences between the experimental and control groups might be due to such changed conditions rather than to the pre-school intervention programme. Put in its most extreme form, this argument would claim that, without the intervention, the 1974 cohort of eight-year-olds in the area would have differed significantly from the 1969 cohort and that our test results reflect this difference. It is true that conditions in the area of the pre-school changed somewhat during the life of the project. Some of the worst housing was demolished and some newer better quality apartments became available. There is also some evidence that reading standards of eleven-year-olds in Dublin city schools improved during the period of the study (McGee, in press). While such factors might suggest differences between the experimental and control groups which are not attributable to the pre-school programme, the evidence is no more than suggestive. In relation to the dependent variables of the present investigation, the pre-school treatment seems the most powerful, relevant and immediate influence characterizing the lives of the experimental group, which was absent from the lives of the control group.

A final point is an extension of the last one in that it also raises questions about the comparability of the experimental and control groups. The control group was made up of a sample of all children aged eight years living in a defined geographical area. The experimental group was made up of all children aged three years living in the same area. In a settled area with little mobility this might not be a problem. However, we know that there was considerable mobility in the area in which this study was carried out. Furthermore, we know that movement was not random, and that there were differences between those who stayed and those who left, particularly in terms of home and personality characteristics. Many of the three-year-olds in the experimental group had left the area by the time they were eight; on the other hand, there were eight-year-olds living in the area that had not been there when the study began. Thus the experimental group at eight years of age is not coterminous with the group of eight-year-olds living in the area.

Alternative approaches to the selection of a control group, however, would have created their own set of problems. For example, the random assignment to experimental and control groups of subjects living within the same area might have seemed preferable. In this kind of situation, however, community and peer group pressures may not operate in the same way in the experimental situation as in ordinary non-experimental conditions. Thus the generalization of the findings becomes a problem (Light and Smith, 1970). Alternatively, a control group might have been selected from a 'similar' area. While this was considered, no obviously comparable area came to mind. Indeed, the criteria one might employ in equating areas were not at all clear. At least in the procedure which we followed, gross environmental conditions were the same for most of the experimental and control subjects; this is something one could not have argued with any degree of confidence had the control group been chosen from a different geographical area.

While doubts may remain, these considerations provide a reasonable basis for confidence in the validity of the design and in the possibility of making inferences about programme effectiveness. There is no way of obtaining absolutely conclusive proof that a particular procedure or programme is effective. At best, one removes alternative explanations for a given effect; this in turn, increases confidence in the effectiveness of the programme that is the subject of investigation (Jones and Borgatta, 1972). On balance, it seems reasonable to conclude from our investigation that the displacement in the rate of development of the experimental children which we observed is attributable to their exposure to the intervention programme. Furthermore, given the nature of the pre-school curriculum and the nature of the criterion measures used in the study, it may be inferred that the curriculum was a major factor in producing the changes in cognitive functioning that were observed during the project.

We cannot, however, on the basis of our findings, unequivocally attribute the observed effects to the pre-school curriculum. We really do not know how the various components of the programme contributed to the attainment of objectives or how these components might have interacted. For example, we do not know how the school-based programme interacted with the home or how that presumed interaction affected the development of the participating children.

Again, while we have evidence to indicate the existence of differences between teachers in programme implementation and of teacher effects, we are not in a position to identify the nature of these differences or effects. While we also know that girls performed better than boys and that less able children seemed to differ from the more able ones in their rates of development during the period of the programme, we are unable to say to what extent such differences reflect differential responses by children to the intervention treatments. There are limitations to the questions any research study can answer and our study was not designed to investigate such issues. This is not to deny their importance for the development of future strategies of intervention. Their investigation, however, will require research and evaluation strategies other than those used in the present study.

The question of external validity — the generalizability of the findings of an experiment — is more difficult than that of external validity. It is one that is never completely answerable (Campbell and Stanley, 1963). In studies of programme evaluation of the kind we are dealing with, since our sample size is really only one, attempts at generalization are indeed hazardous (Jones and Borgatta, 1972). Replications of the project would be required to increase the sample beyond one. In the absence of such replication, generalizations about the suitability of the project for other areas and other conditions must be made with caution. Ultimately, a judgment about the likely suitability of the curriculum used in the present investigation for application in other conditions will depend on the judgment of people who know those conditions well.

Further research

Our findings and their limitations point to the need for further research in a number of crucial areas if future attempts at the development of intervention procedures for children living in disadvantaged backgrounds are to be accompanied by greater success than in the past.

While we have attributed the effects we observed, at least in part, to the curriculum used in the pre-school, our evidence on this point is not conclusive. Neither can we say what elements of the curriculum are most important. In future research, it is of primary importance that greater attempts be made to identify the critical features of relatively successful programmes. This will involve paying more attention to the implementation of programmes, what teachers do in the classroom and how individual children and parents react to intervention procedures.

The investigation of these issues will involve a variety of techniques for data gathering, which as yet have not reached a very high level of development (*cf*. Fullan and Promfret, 1975). Studies carried out in laboratory or quasi-laboratory conditions and which follow strict experimental procedures, in which treatment conditions are varied systematically, may prove of some value, though, it should be borne in mind, there are difficulties in generalizing the findings of strictly controlled experimental studies, which, by their very nature, may appear artificial and unreal to participants. On the other hand, the relative lack of control which the researcher faces in evaluating intervention programmes which are carried out in normal social settings and which have the delivery of a service as their primary aim, can also create serious problems in interpretation. While several methodological suggestions to deal with such problems have been put forward (Campbell, 1969a, 1969b), unresolved issues relating to control and measurement remain. A 'healthy two-way traffic between laboratory and other social settings as alternating sites for experimentation' (R.M. Farr, 1976) seems indicated. While there are precedents for such traffic within the field of social psychology, the recent growth of interest in the application of behavioural science methods and techniques to the solution of social problems has introduced new dimensions to the situation and has resulted in new demands being made on the evaluator and his techniques.

A further issue arising from our findings relates to the fading of the effects of pre-schooling which occurred when children moved to a primary school. This is a phenomenon which has been noted in a number of other studies (*cf*. Bronfenbrenner, 1974) and which has invited a variety of explanations. It may be argued that observed gains at the end of the pre-school should be regarded as unreal or artifactual. However, a number of commentators have pointed to the short length of time a child spends in a pre-school programme and regard it as somewhat unrealistic that such a period should be regarded as sufficient to revolutionize a child's life (*cf*. Karnes, 1973; Stanley, 1973). The fading has also been related to our lack of knowledge regarding intervention at the school level and to difficulties in getting primary schools to experiment with new approaches. For example, it has been argued that the conditions of stimulation in the primary school are less satisfactory for children from disadvantaged backgrounds than are the conditions of the pre-school, the charge being made that primary schools do little to accommodate the interests, values and skills of children from disadvantaged backgrounds. Thus the decline at the later school level, to some extent at any rate, is related to differences between pre-school and later schooling conditions (Little and Smith, 1971). When the intellectual quality of the environment changes, one would expect related changes in the performance of those in the environment (Campbell and Frey, 1970).

In this context, Getzels (1965) has stressed the need to give more thought to the 'transformation' of the school and perhaps less to the transformation of the child. Given the traditions of the primary school and the constraints under which it operates, such a transformation is going to be an arduous task. Indeed it may well be impossible, given the extent of our existing knowledge of the development of children in disadvantaged areas. The need for the extension of that knowledge is very obvious when one comes to plan curricula for such children. This suggests that a high priority should be given to research which will throw light on the environments of disadvantaged children and how development takes place in such environments. Such research would involve studying the abilities, learning styles and personalities of children and how these relate to the culture of the disadvantaged. Its findings should lead to a greater understanding of the dynamics of development in disadvantaged cultures.

An important issue raised by our finding concerns the relationship between skills taught in the pre-school and the demands of the primary school (Bissel, 1973; Tizard, 1974). The programme used in the present investigation was designed to raise the level of general intellectual functioning of participants on the assumption that this would facilitate the acquisition of skills (particularly in reading) traditionally taught in school. The transfer from general cognitive to more specific scholastic skills did not take place to the extent that had been expected. It may be that school failure in disadvantaged children is primarily a motivational and attitudinal problem rather than the effects of language or cognitive deficits (Tizard, 1974; Zigler, 1966). It may also be that in the cognitive area the relationship between intelligence and attainment is not the same for children from disadvantaged backgrounds as it is for the rest of the population (Crano, Kenny and Campbell, 1972; Dyer and Miller, 1974; Kellaghan, 1973). While in the general population, the tendency for intelligence to cause attainment seems stronger than the tendency for attainment to cause intelligence, this tendency has not been found in the case of children living in disadvantaged backgrounds. This suggests that the ability measured by intelligence tests (to employ abstractions, complex rules and schemata) is more likely to result in the acquisition of more concrete information and skills and of the formal attainments of the school (in reading and mathematics) in the case of advantaged than in the case of disadvantaged children. The implications of this situation for the development of curricula in the early years of the primary school for children from disadvantaged backgrounds merit further investigation.

Our relative lack of success to date at the primary school level should not be taken as evidence that successful intervention is not possible with older children. However, as a prerequisite to the development of more effective curricula, a good deal of research will be required on the learning problems of disadvantaged children during the period when they are learning basic skills of literacy and numeracy. The relevance and urgency of the research need hardly be stressed. Reading ability is one of the most important prerequisites for school progress and certain minimum skills are necessary to function comfortably in our society. If children do not acquire basic skills in reading, then the outlook is bleak educationally; they will lack an essential tool for the work of the school and are likely to become frustrated and demoralized.

While the onus for improving the scholastic attainments of children from disadvantaged backgrounds must rest in part on the school, at the same time it should be borne in mind that the reasons for the fading of the early achievements of children from disadvantaged backgrounds may not be found entirely within the school. In view of the strong relationships between home backgrounds of children and their scholastic attainment (Kellaghan, 1976b), the work of the school, it would seem, is likely to be severely limited by the amount of support and cooperation it receives from the home. Research of the kind we are suggesting then will involve a wider context for study than the school. Obviously, it will concern itself with the home, but since, as has been pointed out, poverties have their origins in both situational and cultural characteristics of those minorities which suffer disadvantage and discrimination, remedies will have to be sought in the broad contexts of both economic and cultural (including educational) reform. This may involve not just the local or community level but the total structure of society (Halsey, 1972).

As we move towards a greater understanding of the problems of disadvantage and towards solutions to these problems, we are reminded by Klaus and Gray (1968) of Euclid's words to Alexander — there is no royal road to geometry. 'Just so, there is no quick and easy way to offset the deep and pervasive effects of a deprived environment on a child who has spent 24 hours a day in that environment for four to six years, and whose parents, and often his parents' parents have experienced similar limited environments' (Klaus and Gray, 1968, p. 54). The findings of research to date have brought us part of the way towards understanding and towards dealing with the problems to which life in a disadvantaged environment gives rise. One may hope that, despite its difficulties, the work begun will not now falter for lack of interest, resources or resolve.

REFERENCES

AMERICAN PSYCHOLOGICAL ASSOCIATION, AMERICAN EDU-
CATIONAL RESEARCH ASSOCIATION, NATIONAL COUNCIL
ON MEASUREMENT IN EDUCATION: Joint committee chaired by
Davis, F.B. (1974). *Standards for Educational and Psychological
Tests*. Washington, D.C.: American Psychological Association.

ANASTASI, A. (1968). *Differential Psychology. Individual and Group
Differences in Behavior*. New York: Macmillan.

AUSUBEL, D. and AUSUBEL, P. (1963). 'Ego development among
segregated negro children.' In: PASSOW, A.H. (Ed) *Education in
Depressed Areas*. New York: Teachers College, Columbia University.

AVERCH, H., CARROLL, S.T., DONALDSON, T.S., KIESLING, H.J.,
and PINCUS, J. (1972). *How Effective is Schooling? A critical
review and synthesis of research findings*. Santa Monica, California:
Rand Corporation.

BARNES, J. (1975). *Educational Priority, volume 3: Curriculum
Innovation in London's EPAs*. London: HMSO.

BAYLEY, N. (1970). 'Development of mental abilities.' In:
MUSSEN, P.H. (Ed) *Carmichael's Manual of Child Psychology* (3rd
ed). Volume 1. New York: Wiley.

BEERY, K.E. (1967). *Developmental Test of Visual-Motor Integration.
Administration and Scoring Manual*. Chicago: Follett Educational
Corporation.

BELLER, E.K (1973). 'Research on organized programs of early
education.' In: TRAVERS, R.M.W. (Ed) *Second Handbook of
Research on Teaching*. Chicago: Rand McNally.

BENEDICT, R. (1934). *Patterns of Culture*. Boston: Houghton Mifflin.

BEREITER, C. and ENGELMANN, S. (1966). *Teaching Disadvantaged
Children in the Preschool*. Englewood Cliffs, New Jersey: Prentice—
Hall.

BERNSTEIN, B. (1960). 'Language and social class,' *British Journal of
Sociology*, 11, 271—76.

BERNSTEIN, B. (1961). 'Social class and linguistic development: A
theory of social learning.' In: HALSEY, A.H., FLOUD, J., and
ANDERSON, C.A. (Eds) *Education, Economy and Society*. New
York: Free Press of Glencoe.

BERNSTEIN, B. (1971). *Class, Codes and Control, volume 1: Theoretical Studies towards a Sociology of Language.* London: Routledge and Kegan Paul.

BISSEL, J.S. (1973). 'Planned variation in Head Start and Follow Through.' In: STANLEY, J.S. (Ed) *Compensatory Education for Children ages 2 to 8. Recent Studies of Educational Intervention.* Baltimore: Johns Hopkins University Press.

BLOCK, J., BLOCK, J.H., and HARRINGTON, D.M. (1974) 'Some misgivings about the Matching Familiar Figures Test as a measure of reflection-impulsivity,' *Developmental Psychology*, 10, 611–32.

BLOCK, J., BLOCK, J.H., and HARRINGTON, D.M. (1975). 'Comment on the Kagan–Messer reply,' *Developmental Psychology*, 11, 249–52.

BLOOM, B.S. (1964). *Stability and Change in Human Characteristics.* New York: Wiley.

BLOOM, B.S., DAVIS, A., and HESS, R. (1965). *Contemporary Education for Cultural Deprivation.* New York: Holt, Rinehart and Winston.

BOCK, R.D. and HAGGARD, E.A. (1968). 'The use of multivariate analysis of variance in behavioral research.' In: WHITLA, D. (Ed) *Handbook of Measurement in Education, Psychology and Sociology.* Reading, Mass: Addison–Wesley.

BOYD, J. (1966). *Project Head Start, Summer 1966: Facilities – resources of Head Start centres.* Princeton, New Jersey: Educational Testing Service.

BRIMER, M.A. and DUNN, L.M. (1962). *Manual for the English Picture Vocabulary Test.* Bristol: Educational Evaluation Enterprises.

BRONFENBRENNER, U. (1974). 'Is early intervention effective?' *Teachers College Record*, 76, 279–303.

BRUGHA, D. (1971). A comparative study of disadvantaged and non-disadvantaged eight-year old children in Dublin: Cognitive, scholastic and environmental characteristics. Unpublished MPsychSc thesis, University College, Dublin.

BRUNER, J.S. (1961). 'The cognitive consequences of early sensory deprivation.' In: SOLOMON, P. *et al.* (Eds) *Sensory Deprivation.* Cambridge, Mass.: Harvard University Press.

BURT, C. (1921). *Mental and Scholastic Tests.* London: King.

BURT, C. (1937). *The Backward Child.* London: University of London Press.

CALDWELL, B.M. (1967). *The Preschool Inventory. Directions for administering and scoring.* Princeton, New Jersey: Educational Testing Service.

CAMPBELL, D.T. (1969a). 'Prospective: Artifact and control.' In:

ROSENTHAL, R. and ROSNOW, R.L. (Eds) *Artifact in Behavioral Research*. New York: Academic Press.

CAMPBELL, D.T. (1969b). 'Reforms as experiments,' *American Psychologist*, 24, 409—29.

CAMPBELL, D.T. and ERLEBACHER, A. (1970). 'How regression artifacts in quasi-experimental evaluations can mistakenly make compensatory education look harmful.' In: HELLMUTH, J. (Ed) *Disadvantaged Child, volume 3: Compensatory education: A national debate*. New York: Brunner / Mazel.

CAMPBELL, D.T. and FREY, P.W. (1970). 'The implications of learning theory for the fade-out of gains from compensatory education.' In: HELLMUTH, J. (Ed) *Disadvantaged Child, volume 3: Compensatory education: A national debate*. New York: Brunner / Mazel.

CAMPBELL, D.T. and STANLEY, J.C. (1963). 'Experimental and quasi-experimental designs for research.' In: GAGE, N.L. (Ed) *Handbook of Research on Teaching*. Chicago: Rand McNally.

CARNEY, M. (1970). Maladjustment and disadvantage: A study of maladjustment in a sample of primary school children in an inner-city area in Dublin. Unpublished MPsychSc thesis, University College, Dublin.

CARNEY, M., CHAMBERLAIN, J., GARVEY, C., McGEE, P., and QUINN, P. (1970). Rutland Street research project. Dublin: Department of Psychology, University College, Dublin.

CATTELL, R.B. (1950). *Culture-fair (or free) Intelligence Test. Scale 1: Handbook for the individual or group*. Champaign, Illinois: Institute for Personality and Ability Testing.

CAZDEN, C.B. (1966) 'Cultural differences in child language,' *Merrill-Palmer Quarterly*, 12, 185—220.

CAZDEN, C.B., JOHN, U.P., and HYMES, D. (Eds) (1972). *Functions of Language in the Classroom*. New York: Teachers College Press.

CHAMBERLAIN, J. (1970). Attainment and disadvantage: A study of the relationship between school attainment and disadvantage in a Dublin inner-city sub-culture. Unpublished MPsychSc thesis, University College, Dublin.

CHAZAN, M. (1973). 'The concept of compensatory education.' In: CHAZAN, M. (Ed) *Compensatory Education*. London: Butterworths.

CHAZAN, M., LAING, A., and JACKSON, S. (1971). *Just before School*. Oxford: Blackwell.

CICIRELLI, V.G. (1970). 'The relevance of the regression artifact problem to the Westinghouse—Ohio evaluation of Head Start: A reply to Campbell and Erlebacher.' In: HELLMUTH, J. (Ed) *Disadvantaged Child, volume 3: Compensatory education: A national debate*. New York: Brunner / Mazel.

CICIRELLI, V.G., EVANS, J.W., and SCHILLER, J.S. (1970). 'The impact of Head Start: A reply to the report analysis,' *Harvard Educational Review*, 40, 105–29.

CLYMER, T. and BARRETT, T.C. (1968). *Clymer-Barrett Prereading Battery. Directions Manual Form A*. Lexington, Mass.: Personnel Press.

COLEMAN, J.S. (1968). 'The concept of equality of educational opportunity,' *Harvard Educational Review*, 38, 7–22.

COLEMAN, J.S., CAMPBELL, E.Q., HOBSON, C.J., McPARTLAND, J., MOOD, A.M., WEINFELD, F.D., and YORK, R.L. (1966). *Equality of Educational Opportunity*. Washington, D.C.: Office of Education, US Department of Health, Education and Welfare.

COOLEY, W.W. (1974). 'Assessment of educational effects,' *Educational Psychologist*, 11, 29–35.

COOLEY, W.W. and LOHNES, P.R. (1962). *Multivariate Procedures for the Behavioral Sciences*. New York: Wiley.

COOLEY, W.W. and LOHNES, P.R. (1971). *Multivariate Data Analysis*. New York: Wiley.

COUNCIL OF EUROPE. Documentation Centre for Education in Europe (1971a). *A Documentary Report on Recent Research into Preschool Education*. Strasbourg: Council of Europe.

COUNCIL OF EUROPE. Documentation Centre for Education in Europe (1971b). *Research into Preschool Education*. Strasbourg: Council of Europe.

COUNCIL OF EUROPE. Documentation Centre for Education in Europe (1974). *Information Bulletin*, No. 1.

CRANO, W.D., KENNY, D.A., and CAMPBELL, D.T. (1972). 'Does intelligence cause achievement? A cross-lagged panel analysis,' *Journal of Educational Psychology*, 63, 258–57.

CRONBACH, L.J. (1969). 'Heredity, environment and educational policy,' *Harvard Educational Review*, 39, 338–47.

CRUICKSHANK, W.M. and QUALTERE, T.J. (1950). 'The use of intelligence tests with children of retarded mental development: 11. Clinical considerations,' *American Journal of Mental Deficiency*, 54, 370–381.

CULLEN, K. (1969). *School and Family. Social factors in educational attainment*. Dublin: Gill and Macmillan.

DATTA, L.E. (1975). 'Design of the Head Start Planned Variation experiment.' In: RIVLIN, A.M. and TIMPANE, P.M. (Eds) *Planned Variation in Education. Should we give up or try harder?* Washington, D.C.: Brookings Institution.

DAVE, R.H. (1963). The identification and measurement of environmental process variables related to educational achievement.

Unpublished PhD thesis, University of Chicago.

DEUTSCH, M. (1963). 'The disadvantaged child and the learning process: Some social, psychological and developmental considerations.' In: PASSOW, A.H. (Ed) *Education in Depressed Areas.* New York: Teachers College Bureau of Publications.

DEUTSCH, M. (1967). 'The social environment for learning.' In: DEUTSCH, M. *et al.,* (Eds) *The Disadvantaged Child.* New York: Basic Books.

DI LORENZO, L.T. and SALTER, R. (1968). 'An evaluative study of pre-kindergarten programs for educationally disadvantaged children,' *Exceptional Children,* **35**, 111—19.

DI LORENZO, L.T., SALTER, R., and BRADY, J. (1969). *Pre-kindergarten Programs for Educationally Disadvantaged Children.* Final Report, Project No. 3040. Washington, D.C.: US Office of Education.

DOUGLAS, J.W.B. (1964). *The Home and the School.* London: McGibbon and Kee.

DUNCAN, O.D. (1969). 'Inheritance of poverty or inheritance of race.' In: MOYNIHAN, D.P. (Ed) *On Understanding Poverty.* New York: Basic Books.

DYER, J.L. and MILLER, L.B. (1974). 'Note on Crano, Kenny and Campbell's "Does intelligence cause achievement?"', *Journal of Educational Psychology,* **66**, 49—51.

EDWARDS, A.D. (1974). 'Social class and linguistic inference,' *Research in Education,* **12**, 71—80.

EELLS, K., DAVIS, A., HAVIGHURST, R.J., MERRICK, V.E., and TYLER, R. (1951). *Intelligence and Cultural Differences.* Chicago: University of Chicago Press.

EISENBERG, L. (1963). 'Strengths of the inner city child,' *Baltimore Bulletin of Education,* **41**, 10—16.

ELKIND, D. (1969). 'Piagetian and psychometric conceptions of intelligence,' *Harvard Educational Review,* **39**, 319—37.

EVANS, J.W., and SCHILLER, J. (1970). 'How preoccupation with possible regression artifacts can lead to a faulty strategy for the evaluation of social action programs: A reply to Campbell and Erlebacher.' In: HELLMUTH, J. (Ed) *Disadvantaged Child, volume 3: Compensatory education: A national debate.* New York: Brunner / Mazel.

FANTINI, M.D. (1969). 'Beyond cultural deprivation and compensatory education,' *Psychiatry and Social Science Review,* **3**, 6—13.

FANTINI, M.D. and WEINSTEIN, G. (1968). *The Disadvantaged: Challenge to education.* New York: Harper and Row.

FARR, R. (1972). 'Review of Clymer-Barrett Prereading Battery.' In: BUROS, O. (Ed) *The Seventh Mental Measurements Yearbook,*

Volume II. Highland Park, New Jersey: Gryphon Press.

FARR, R.M. (1976). 'Experimentation: A social psychological perspective,' *British Journal of Social and Clinical Psychology*, 15, 225—38.

FERMAN, L.A., KORNBLUH, J.L., and HABER, A. (1965). 'Introduction to definitions and prevalence of poverty.' In: FERMAN, L.A., KORNBLUH, J.L., and HABER, A. (Eds) *Poverty in America: A book of readings*. Ann Arbor, Michigan: University of Michigan.

FLAVELL, J.H., BOTKIN, P.T., FRY, C.L., WRIGHT, J.W., and JARVIS, P.E. (1968). *The Development of Role-taking and Communication Skills in Children*. New York: Wiley.

FLOUD, J., HALSEY, A.H., and MARTIN, F.M. (1957). *Social Class and Educational Opportunity*. London: Heinemann.

FRASER, E.D. (1959). *Home Environment and the School*. London: University of London Press.

FREEBURG, N.E. and PAYNE, D.T. (1967), 'Dimensions of parental practice concerned with cognitive development in the preschool child,' *Journal of Genetic Psychology*, 111, 245—61.

FREEMAN, F.N. and FLORY, C.D. (1937). 'Growth in intellectual ability as measured by repeated tests,' *Monographs of the Society for Research in Child Development*, 2, (2, Serial No. 9).

FULLAN, M. and PROMFRET, A. (1975). Review of research on curriculum implementation. Report prepared for Career Development Program, National Institute for Education, Washington NIE—P—74—0122. Toronto: Ontario Institute for Studies in Education.

GALLAGHER, J.J. (1968). 'The disadvantaged gifted.' In: TANNENBAUM, A.J. (Ed) *Special Education and Programs for Disadvantaged Children and Youth*. Washington, D.C.: Council for Exceptional Children.

GANS, H. (1962). *The Urban Villagers*. New York: Free Press.

GETZELS, J.W. (1965). 'Preschool education.' In: *Contemporary Issues in American Education*. Papers prepared for the White House Conference on Education, Washington, D.C., July 1965.

GINSBURG, H. (1972). *The Myth of the Deprived Child: Poor children's intellect and education*. Englewood Cliffs, New Jersey: Prentice-Hall.

GLICK, J. (1968). 'Some problems in the evaluation of pre-school intervention programs.' In: HESS, R.D. and BEAR, R.M. (Eds) *Early Education. Current theory, research, and action*. Chicago: Aldine.

GOLDSCHMIDT, D. and SOMMERKORN, I.N. (1970). 'Deprivation and disadvantage: Federal Republic of Germany.' In: PASSOW, A.H. (Ed) *Deprivation and Disadvantage: Nature and manifestations*. Hamburg: UNESCO Institute for Education.

GORDON, E.W. (1970). 'Introduction to education for socially disadvantaged children,' *Review of Educational Research*, **40**, 1—12.

GORDON, E.W. and WILKERSON, D.A. (1966). *Compensatory education for the disadvantaged. Programs and practices. Preschool through college*. New York: College Entrance Examination Board.

GORDON, I.J. (1971). *A Home Learning Approach to Early Stimulation*. Gainesville, Fla: University of Florida, Institute for Development of Human Resources.

GORDON, I.J. (1973). *An Early Intervention Project: A longitudinal look*. Gainesville, Fla: University of Florida, Institute for Development of Human Resources.

GORDON, I.J. (1975). *The Infant Experience*. Columbus, Ohio: Charles E. Merrill.

GORDON, J.E. (1968). 'The disadvantaged pupil,' *Irish Journal of Education*, **2**, 69—105.

GRAY, S. and KLAUS, R.A. (1970). 'The early training project: A seventh-year report,' *Child Development*, **41**, 909—24.

GREAT BRITAIN: DEPARTMENT OF EDUCATION AND SCIENCE (1967). *Children and their Primary Schools. A report of the Central Advisory Council for Education (England)*. London: HMSO.

GREAT BRITAIN: REGISTRAR GENERAL (1956). *Census 1951: Classification of occupations*. London: HMSO.

HALLIDAY, M.A.K. (1973). 'The functional basis of language.' In: BERNSTEIN, B. (Ed) *Class, Codes and Control, volume 2: Applied studies towards a sociology of language*. London: Routledge and Kegan Paul.

HALSEY, A.H. (Ed) (1972). *Educational Priority, volume 1: EPA problems and policies*. London: HMSO.

HAVIGHURST, R.J. (1970). 'Deprivation and disadvantage: USA.' In: PASSOW, A.H. (Ed) *Deprivation and Disadvantage: Nature and Manifestations*. Hamburg: UNESCO Institute for Education.

HAWKRIDGE, D.G., CHALUPSKY, A.B., and ROBERTS, A.O.H. (1968). *A study of selected exemplary programs for the education of disadvantaged children*. Washington, D.C.: US Department of Health, Education and Welfare.

HAWKRIDGE, D.G., TALLMADGE, G.K., and LARSEN, J.K. (1968). *Foundations for Success in Educating Disadvantaged Children*. Washington, D.C.: US Department of Health, Education, and Welfare.

HEBB, D.O. (1949). *The Organization of Behavior*. New York: Wiley.

HENRY, J. (1971). *Essays on Education*. Harmondsworth: Penguin.

HESS, R.D. and SHIPMAN, V.C. (1965). 'Early experience and the socialization of cognitive modes in children,' *Child Development*, **36**, 869—886.

HESS, R.D. and SHIPMAN, V.C. (1967). 'Cognitive elements in

maternal behavior.' In: HILL, J.P. (Ed) *Minnesota Symposia on Child Psychology, volume 1*. Minneapolis: University of Minnesota Press.

HUNT, J.McV. (1969). 'Has compensatory education failed? Has it been attempted?' *Harvard Educational Review*, **39**, 278—300.

HUSEN, T. (1969). *Talent, Opportunity and Career*. Stockholm: Almqvist and Wiksell.

INSTITUTE FOR DEVELOPMENTAL STUDIES (nd). *Children's Behavior Rating Scale*. New York: Department of Psychiatry, New York Medical College.

INVESTMENT IN EDUCATION (1966). Report of the Survey Team appointed by the Minister for Education in October, 1962. Dublin: Stationery Office.

IRELAND: CENTRAL STATISTICS OFFICE (1970). *Census of Population of Ireland, 1966, volume vii: Education*. Dublin: Stationery Office.

IRELAND: COMMISSION OF INQUIRY ON MENTAL HANDICAP (1966). *Report*. Dublin: Stationery Office.

JENCKS, C.S., SMITH, M., ACLAND, H., BANE, M.J., COHEN, D., GINTIS, H., HEYNS, B., and MICHELSON, S. (1972). *Inequality: A reassessment of the effect of family and schooling in America*. New York: Basic Books.

JENSEN, A.R. (1967). 'The culturally disadvantaged: Psychological and educational aspects,' *Educational Research*, **10**, 4—20.

JENSEN, A.R. (1968). 'Social class and verbal learning.' In: DEUTSCH, M., KATZ, I., and JENSEN, A.R. (Eds) *Social Class, Race and Psychological Development*. New York: Holt, Rinehart and Winston.

JENSEN, A.R. (1969). 'How much can we boost IQ and scholastic achievement?' *Harvard Educational Review*, **39**, 1—123.

JENSEN, A.R. (1972). *Genetics and Education*. New York: Harper and Row.

JENSEN, A.R. (1973). *Educability and Group Differences*. London: Methuen.

JONES, P.A. and McMILLAN, W.B. (1973). 'Speech characteristics as a function of social class and situational factors,' *Child Development*, **44**, 117—21.

JONES, W.C. and BORGATTA, E.F. (1972). 'Methodology of evaluation.' In: MULLEN, E.J., DUMPSON, J.R., and Associates (Eds) *Evaluation of Social Intervention*. San Francisco: Jossey-Bass.

KAGAN, J. (1965). 'Reflection-impulsivity and reading ability in primary grade children,' *Child Development*, **36**, 609—28.

KAGAN, J. (1967). 'Biological aspects of inhibition systems,' *American Journal of Diseases of Children*, **114**, 507—12.

KAGAN, J. (1969). 'Inadequate evidence and illogical conclusions,' *Harvard Educational Review*, 39, 274—77.

KAGAN, J. and MESSER, S.B. (1975). 'A reply to "Some misgivings about the Matching Familiar Figures Test as a measure of reflection-impulsivity",' *Developmental Psychology*, 11, 244—48.

KAGAN, J., ROSMAN, B., DAY, D., ALBERT, J., and PHILLIPS, W. (1964). 'Information-processing in the child: Significance of analytic and reflective attitudes,' *Psychological Monographs, General and Applied*, 78 (Whole No. 578).

KAHL, J.A. and DAVIS, J.A. (1955). 'A comparison of indexes of socioeconomic status,' *American Sociological Review*, 20, 317—25.

KAMII, C.K. (1970). A sketch of the Piaget derived preschool curriculum developed by the Ypsilanti early education program. Ypsilanti, Michigan: Ypsilanti Public Schools.

KAMII, C.K. (1971). 'Objectives of preschool education.' In: BLOOM, B.S., HASTINGS, J.T., and MADAUS, G.F. (Eds) *Handbook on Formative and Summative Evaluation of Student Learning*. New York: McGraw-Hill.

KAMII, C.K., and RADIN, N.L. (1970). 'A framework for a preschool curriculum based on some Piagetian concepts.' In: ATHEY, I.J. and RUBADEAU, D.O. (Eds) *Educational Implications of Piaget's Theory*. Waltham, Mass.: Ginn-Blaisdell.

KAPLAN, J.L. and MANDEL, S. (1969). 'Class differences in the effects of impulsivity, goal orientation and verbal expression on an object-sorting task,' *Child Development*, 40, 491—502.

KARNES, M.B. (1969). *Research and Development Program on Preschool Disadvantaged Children: Final Report*. Washington, D.C.: US Office of Education.

KARNES, M.B. (1973). 'Evaluation and implications of research with young handicapped and low-income children.' In: STANLEY, J.C. (Ed) *Compensatory Education for Children ages 2 to 8. Recent Studies of Educational Intervention*. Baltimore: Johns Hopkins University Press.

KATZ, P.A. and DEUTSCH, M. (1967). 'The relationship of auditory and visual functioning to reading achievement in disadvantaged children.' In: DEUTSCH, M. *et al.* (Eds) *The Disadvantaged Child*. New York: Basic Books.

KELLAGHAN, T. (1968). 'Abstraction and categorization in African children,' *International Journal of Psychology*, 3, 115—20.

KELLAGHAN, T. (1970). 'Deprivation and disadvantage in Ireland.' In: PASSOW, A.H. (Ed) *Deprivation and Disadvantage: Nature and manifestations*. Hamburg: UNESCO Institute for Education.

KELLAGHAN, T. (1971). A preschool project in a disadvantaged area in Dublin. Paper presented at Seminar on Early Childhood

Education in the Caribbean. Kingston, Jamaica, 4—9 October.

KELLAGHAN, T. (1972). 'Preschool intervention for the educationally disadvantaged,' *Irish Journal of Psychology*, 1, 160—76.

KELLAGHAN, T. (1973). 'Intelligence and achievement in a disadvantaged population: A cross-lagged panel analysis,' *Irish Journal of Education*, 7, 23—28.

KELLAGHAN, T. (1975). The evaluation of a preschool programme for disadvantaged children. Report submitted to the Department of Education, Dublin and The Van Leer Foundation, The Hague. Dublin: Educational Research Centre, St Patrick's College, Dublin.

KELLAGHAN, T. (1976a). 'Learning disabilities in Ireland.' In: TARNOPOL, L. (Ed) *Reading Disabilities: An international perspective*. Baltimore: University Park Press.

KELLAGHAN, T. (1976b). Relationships between home environment and scholastic behaviour. Unpublished manuscript.

KELLAGHAN, T. and ARCHER, P. (1973). A home intervention project for two- and three-year-old disadvantaged children. Dublin: Educational Research Centre, St Patrick's College, Dublin.

KELLAGHAN, T. and BRUGHA, A. (1972). 'The scholastic performance of children in a disadvantaged area,' *Irish Journal of Education*, 6, 133—43.

KELLAGHAN, T. and GREANEY, B.J. (1973). 'A factorial study of the characteristics of preschool disadvantaged children,' *Irish Journal of Education*, 7, 55—65.

KELLAGHAN, T. and GREANEY, V. (1970). 'Factors related to choice of post-primary school in Ireland,' *Irish Journal of Education*, 4, 69—83.

KELLAGHAN, T. and MACNAMARA, J. (1972). 'Family correlates of verbal reasoning ability,' *Developmental Psychology*, 7, 49—53.

KELLAGHAN, T. and O hUALLACHAIN, S. (1969). 'A project for disadvantaged preschool children,' *Oideas*, 3, 28—32.

KELLAGHAN, T. and O hUALLACHAIN, S. (1973). 'A preschool intervention project for disadvantaged children,' *Oideas*, 10, 38—47.

KELLY, S. (1970). *Teaching in the City. A study of the role of the primary teacher*. Dublin: Gill and Macmillan.

KELLY, S. and McGEE, P. (1967). 'Survey of reading comprehension: A study in Dublin city national schools,' *New Research in Education*, 1, 131—34.

KESSEL, F.S. (1974). 'Pre-schooling' for the disadvantaged: The interplay of social policy, scientific theory and educational practice. The Hague: Bernard Van Leer Foundation.

KIRK, S.A., McCARTHY, J.J., and KIRK, W.D. (1968). *Illinois Test of Psycholinguistic Abilities. Examiner's Manual*. (Revised edition). Urbana, Ill.: University of Illinois Press.

KLAUS, R.A. and GRAY, S.W. (1968). 'The early training project for disadvantaged children: A report after five years,' *Monographs of the Society for Research in Child Development*, **33**, (4, Whole No. 120).

KLUCKHOHN, F.R. and STRODTBECK, F.L. (1961). *Variations in Value Orientations*. Chicago: Row, Peterson.

KOHLBERG, L. (1968). 'Montessori with the culturally disadvantaged.' In: HESS, R.D. and BEAR, R.M. (Eds) *Early Education. Current theory, research and action*. Chicago: Aldine.

KRAUSS, R.M. and ROTTER, G.S. (1968). 'Communication abilities of children as a function of status and age,' *Merrill-Palmer Quarterly*, **14**, 161–74.

LABOV, W. (1969). 'The logic of nonstandard English,' *Georgetown Monographs on Language and Linguistics*, **22**, 1–31.

LABOV, W. (1972). 'The study of language in its social context.' In: GIGLIOLI, P. (Ed) *Language and Social Context*. Harmondsworth: Penguin.

LESSER, G.S., FIFER, G., and CLARK, D.H. (1965). 'Mental abilities of children from different social class and cultural groups,' *Monographs for the Society for Research in Child Development*, **30** (4, Serial No. 102).

LEWIS, O. (1969). 'The culture of poverty.' In: MOYNIHAN, D.P. (Ed) *On Understanding Poverty*. New York: Basic Books.

LIGHT, R.H. and SMITH, P.V. (1970). 'Choosing a future: Strategies for designing and evaluating new programs,' *Harvard Educational Review*, **40**, 1–28.

LITTLE, A. and SMITH, G. (1971). *Strategies of Compensation: A review of educational projects for the disadvantaged in the United States*. Paris: Organisation for Economic Co-operation and Development.

LOHNES, P.R. (1966). 'Nature of the TALENT variables and methods of the studies.' In: FLANAGAN, J.C. and COOLEY, W.W. (Eds) *Project TALENT: One-year follow-up studies*. Co-operative Research Project Number 2333. Pittsburgh: School of Education, University of Pittsburgh.

MACCOBY, E.E. (Ed) (1967). *The Development of Sex Differences*. London: Tavistock Publications.

MacDONALD, R. (1971). Factor analysis of the Appalachia Preschool Education Program test data. Washington, D.C.: Office of Education, US Department of Health, Education and Welfare. (ERIC Document Reproduction Service No. ED 062 020)

MACNAMARA, J. (1966). *Bilingualism and Primary Education*. Edinburgh: Edinburgh University Press.

MADAUS, G.F. and ELMORE, R. (1973). Testimony submitted to the Education and Labor Committee of the House of Representatives on

Bill HR 5163. Huron Institute, Harvard University, Mimeographed.

MADAUS, G.F., KELLAGHAN, T., and RAKOW, E. (1975). A study of the sensitivity of measures of school effectiveness. Report submitted to the Carnegie Corporation, New York. Dublin: Educational Research Centre, St Patrick's College.

MARJORIBANKS, K., (1974a). 'Environment, social class and mental abilities.' In: MARJORIBANKS, K. (Ed) *Environments for Learning.* Slough: NFER.

MARJORIBANKS, K. (1974b). 'Environmental correlates of ability: A canonical analysis.' In: MARJORIBANKS, K. (Ed) *Environments for Learning.* Slough: NFER.

MAYER, R.S. (1971). 'A comparative analysis of preschool curriculum models.' In: ANDERSON, R.H. and SHANE, H.G. (Eds) *As the Twig is Bent. Readings in early childhood education.* Boston: Houghton Mifflin.

McDILL, E.L., McDILL, M.S., and SPREHE, J.T. (1969) *Strategies for Success in Compensatory Education: An appraisal of evaluation research.* Baltimore: Johns Hopkins Press.

McDILL, E.L., McDILL, M.S., and SPREHE, J.T. (1972). 'Evaluation in practice: Compensatory education.' In: ROSSI, P.H. and WILLIAMS, W. (Eds) *Evaluating Social Programs: Theory, practice and politics.* New York: Seminar Press.

McGEE, P. (1970). Intelligence and disadvantage: A study of the levels of schoolchildren's intelligence and of the relationship between intelligence and home environment in a disadvantaged area in Dublin: Unpublished MPsychSc thesis, University College, Dublin.

McGEE, P. (in press). 'An examination of trends in reading achievement in Dublin over a ten-year period.' In: GREANEY, V. (Ed) *Studies in Reading.* Dublin: Educational Company of Ireland.

McKAY, H., McKAY, A., and SINISTERRA, L. (1973). Stimulation of intellectual and social competence in Colombian preschool children affected by the multiple deprivations of depressed urban environments. Cali, Columbia: Fundacion Estacion de Investigaciones de Ecologia Humana.

McNEMAR, Q. (1942). *The Revision of the Stanford—Binet Scale: An analysis of the standardization data.* Boston: Houghton Mifflin.

MIDWINTER, E. (1972). *Priority Education. An account of the Liverpool project.* Harmondsworth: Penguin.

MILLER, S., RIESSMAN, F., and SEAGULL, A. (1965). 'Poverty and self-indulgence: A critique of the non-deferred gratification pattern.' In: FERMAN, O.L., KORNBLUH, J., and HABER, A. (Eds) *Poverty in America.* Ann Arbor, Michigan: University of Michigan Press.

MILNER, E. (1949). 'Effects of sex role and social status on the early adolescent personality,' *Genetic Psychology Monographs*, 40, 231—325.

MISCHEL, W. (1961). 'Preferences for delayed reinforcement and social responsibility,' *Journal of Abnormal and Social Psychology*, **62**, 1–7.

MORIARTY, A.E. (1966). *Constancy and IQ Change: A clinical view of the relationships between tested intelligence and personality*. Springfield, Ill.: Thomas.

MORRISON, C.M., WATT, J.S., and LEE, T.R. (Eds) (1974). *Educational Priority, volume 5: EPA — a Scottish study*. Edinburgh: HMSO.

MOSS, M.H. (1973). *Deprivation and Disadvantage?* Bletchley, Bucks: Open University Press.

MOUNTFORD, J. (1970). 'Some psycholinguistic components of initial standard literacy,' *Journal of Typographic Research*, **4**, 295–306.

NISBET, J. (1970). 'Deprivation and disadvantage: Scotland.' In: PASSOW, A.H. (Ed) *Deprivation and Disadvantage: Nature and manifestations*. Hamburg: UNESCO Institute for Education.

OLIM, E.G., HESS, R.D., and SHIPMAN, V.C. (1967). 'Role of mothers' language styles in mediating their preschool children's cognitive development,' *School Review*, **75**, 414–24.

O SUILLEABHAIN, S.V. (1970). *Marino Graded Word Reading Scale*. Dublin: Longmans, Browne and Nolan.

PARSONS, T. (1959). 'The school class as a social system: Some of its functions in American society,' *Harvard Educational Review*, **29**, 297–318.

PASSOW, A.H. (Ed) (1970). *Deprivation and Disadvantage: Nature and manifestations*. Hamburg: UNESCO Institute for Education.

PASSOW, A.H. and ELLIOT, D.L. (1967). 'The disadvantaged in depressed areas.' In: WITTY, P.A. (Ed) *The Educationally Retarded and Disadvantaged*. Sixty-sixth Yearbook of the National Society for the Study of Education, Part I. Chicago: National Society for the Study of Education.

PASSOW, A.H. and ELLIOT, D.L. (1968). 'The nature and needs of the educationally disadvantaged.' In: PASSOW, A.H. (Ed) *Developing Programs for the Educationally Disadvantaged*. New York: Teachers College Press.

PAYNE, J. (1974). *Educational Priority, volume 2: EPA surveys and statistics*. London: HMSO.

PEAKER, J.F. (1967). 'The regression analysis of the National Survey, Appendix 4.' In: GREAT BRITAIN: DEPARTMENT OF EDUCATION AND SCIENCE. *Children and their Primary Schools, volume 2: Research and surveys*. London: HMSO.

PIAGET, J. (1950). *The Psychology of Intelligence*. London: Routledge and Kegan Paul.

PIAGET, J. (1959). *The Psychology and Thought of the Child*.

London: Routledge and Kegan Paul.

PINNEAU, S.R. (1961). *Changes in Intelligence Quotient. Infancy to Maturity*. Boston: Houghton Mifflin.

PORTEUS, S.D. (1939). 'Racial group differences in mentality,' *Tabulae Biologicae*, **18**, 66—75.

POSNER, J. (1968). Evaluation of 'successful' projects in compensatory education. Washington, D.C.: US Office of Education, Office of Planning and Evaluation. Occasional Paper No. 8.

RADIN, N. and KAMII, C.K. (1965). 'The child-rearing attitudes of disadvantaged negro mothers and some educational implications,' *Journal of Negro Education*, **34**, 138—46.

RIESSMAN, F. (1962). *The Culturally Deprived Child*. New York: Harper and Row.

ROMAN, K. (1974). 'A review of pre-school experiments and research in Finland,' *Paedagogica Europaea*, **9**, (1), 163—71.

RULON, P.J. and BROOKS, W.D. (1968). 'On statistical tests of group differences.' In: WHITLA, D.K. (Ed) *Handbook of Measurement and Assessment in Behavioral Sciences*. Reading, Mass.: Addison-Wesley.

Scala Gradaithe sa Gaeilge (Leamh) (1969). Dublin: Educational Research Centre, St Patrick's College.

SCHOOLS COUNCIL (1968). *Project in Compensatory Education*. Field Report No. 6. London: Schools Council.

SEARS, P.S. and DOWLEY, E.M. (1963). 'Research on teaching in the nursery school.' In: GAGE, N.L. (Ed) *Handbook of Research on Teaching*. Chicago: Rand McNally.

SIEGEL, S. (1956). *Nonparametric Statistics for the Behavioral Sciences*. New York: McGraw-Hill.

SILBERBERG, M., IVERSEN, I., and SILBERBERG, M. (1968). 'The predictive efficiency of the Gates Reading Readiness Tests,' *Elementary School Journal*, **68**, 213—18.

SMILANSKY, S. (1968). *The Effects of Sociodramatic Play on Disadvantaged Preschool Children*. New York: Wiley.

SMITH, G. (Ed) (1975). *Educational Priority, volume 4: The West Riding EPA*. London: HMSO.

SMITH, K.J. (1972). 'Review of Clymer—Barrett Prereading Battery.' In: BUROS, O. (Ed) *The Seventh Mental Measurements Yearbook. volume II*. Highland Park, New Jersey: Gryphon Press.

SMITH, M.S. (1975). 'Evaluation findings in Head Start Planned Variation.' In: RIVLIN, A.M. and TIMPANE, P.M. (Eds) *Planned Variation in Education. Should we give up or try harder?* Washington, D.C.: Brookings Institution.

SMITH, M.S. and BISSELL, J.S. (1970). 'Report analysis: The impact of Head Start,' *Harvard Educational Review*, **40**, 51—104.

SOAR, R.S. and SOAR, R.M. (1972). 'An empirical analysis of selected follow-through programs: An example of the process approach to evaluation.' In: GORDON, I.J. (Ed) *Early Childhood Education*. Seventy-first Yearbook of the National Society for the Study of Education, Part II. Chicago: National Society for the Study of Education.

SOCIAL SCIENCE RESEARCH COUNCIL (1968). *Research on Poverty*. London: Heinemann.

SONQUIST, H., KAMII, C.K., and DERMAN, L. (1970). 'A Piaget-derived preschool curriculum.' In: ATHY, I.J. and RUBADEAU, D.O. (Eds) *Educational Implications of Piaget's Theory*. Waltham, Mass.: Ginn—Blaisdell.

SONTAG, L.W., BAKER, C.T., and NELSON, V.L. (1958). 'Mental growth and personality development: A longitudinal study,' *Monographs of the Society for Research in Child Development*, 23 (2, Whole No. 68).

SROUFE, L.A. (1970). 'A methodological and philosophical critique of intervention-oriented research,' *Developmental Psychology*, 2, 140—145.

STANLEY, J.C. (1973). 'Introduction and critique.' In: STANLEY, J.C. (Ed) *Compensatory Education for Children ages 2 to 8: Recent studies of educational intervention*. Baltimore: Johns Hopkins University Press.

STERN, C. (1967a). *The Children's Auditory Discrimination Inventory*. Los Angeles: UCLA Research Projects in Early Childhood Learning.

STERN, C. (1967b). *Visual Discrimination Inventory*. Los Angeles: UCLA Research Projects in Early Childhood Learning.

STERN, C. (1968). 'Evaluating language criteria for pre-school children.' In: BROTTMAN, M.A. (Ed) Language remediation for the disadvantaged pre-school child. *Monographs of the Society for Research in Child Development*, 33 (8, Serial No. 124).

STODOLSKY, S. (1972). 'Defining treatment and outcome in early-childhood education.' In: WALBERG, H.J. and KOPAN, A.T. (Eds) *Rethinking Urban Education*. San Francisco: Jossey—Bass.

STUFFLEBEAM, D.L., FOLEY, W.J., GEPHART, W.J., GUBA, E.G., HAMMOND, R.I., MERRIMAN, H.O., and PROVUS, M.M. (1971). *Educational Evaluation and Decision Making*. Itasca, Ill.: Peacock.

STUKÁT, K.G. (1974a). 'Current trends in European pre-school research with particular regard to compensatory education,' *Information Bulletin of the Council of Europe*, 1, 77—83.

STUKÁT, K.G. (1974b). 'Research on pre-school programs in Sweden,' *Paedagogica Europaea*, 9, (1), 75—86.

SUSSMAN, L. (1967). Summary review by the rapporteur. In: OECD: Study group in the Economics of Education and Educational

Investment and Planning programme. *Social Objectives in Educational Planning*. Paris: Organisation for Economic Co-operation and Development.

SWIFT, J.W. (1964). 'Effects of early group experience: The nursery school and day nursery.' In: HOFFMAN, M.L. and HOFFMAN, L.W. (Eds) *Review of Child Development Research, volume 1*. New York: Russell Sage Foundation.

TATSUOKA, M.M. (1970). *Discriminant Analysis. The study of group differences*. Champaign, Ill.: Institute for Personality and Ability Testing.

TATSUOKA, M.M. (1971). *Multivariate Analysis: Techniques for educational and psychological research*. New York: Wiley.

TELEGDY, G.A. (1974). 'A factor analysis of four school readiness tests,' *Psychology in the Schools*, 11, 127—133.

TELEGDY, G.A. (1975). 'The effectiveness of four readiness tests as predictors of first grade academic achievement,' *Psychology in the Schools*, 12, 4—11.

TERMAN, L.M. and MERRILL, M.A. (1961). *Stanford—Binet Intelligence Scale. Manual for the third revision Form L—M*. London: Harrap.

THIRION, A.M. (1974). 'Evaluation of compensatory education programmes,' *Information Bulletin of the Council of Europe*, 1, 23—31.

THOMPSON, C.W. and MAGARET, A. (1947). 'Differential test responses of normals and mental defectives,' *Journal of Abnormal and Social Psychology*, 42, 284—93.

TIZARD, B. (1974). *Early Childhood Education. A review and discussion of research in Britain*. Slough: NFER.

TORRANCE, E.P. (1974). 'Differences are not deficits,' *Teachers College Record*, 75, 471—88.

TOUGH, J. (1973a). *Focus on Meaning. Talking to some purpose with young children*. London: Allen and Unwin.

TOUGH, J. (1973b). 'The language of young children.' In: CHAZAN, M. (Ed) *Education in the Early Years*. Swansea: Faculty of Education, University College of Swansea.

TULKIN, S.R. (1972). 'An analysis of the concept of cultural deprivation,' *Developmental Psychology*, 6, 326—39.

TURNER, I.F. (in press). 'Cognitive effects of playgroup attendance,' *Irish Journal of Education*.

VALETT, R.E. (1965). Stanford—Binet L—M item classifications. Palo Alto, California: Consulting Psychologists Press.

VAN ALSTYNE, D. (1929). *The Environment of Three-year old Children. Factors related to intelligence and vocabulary tests*. New York: Teachers College, Columbia University.

VAN LEER FOUNDATION (1971). *Compensatory Early Childhood*

Education: A selective working bibliography. The Hague: Bernard Van Leer Foundation.

VERNON, M.D. (1957). *Backwardness in Reading*. Cambridge: University Press.

VERNON, P.E. (1961). *Intelligence and Attainment Tests*. London: University of London Press.

WEIKART, D.P. (Ed) (1967). Preschool intervention: A preliminary report of the Perry Preschool Project. Ann Arbor, Michigan: Campus Publishers.

WEIKART, D.P. (1969). A comparative study of three preschool curricula. Paper presented at biennial meeting of the Society for Research in Child Development, Santa Monica, California.

WEIKART, D.P. (1971). Relationship of curriculum, teaching and learning in preschool education. Paper presented at the Human Blumberg Memorial Symposium on Research in Early Childhood Education, The Johns Hopkins University.

WEIKART, D.P. (1972). 'Relationship of curriculum, teaching, and learning in preschool education.' In: STANLEY, J.S. (Ed) *Preschool Programs for the Disadvantaged: Five experimental approaches to early education*. Baltimore: Johns Hopkins University Press.

WEIKART, D.P., DELORIA, D.J., LAWSER, S.A., and WEIGERINK, R. (1970). *Longitudinal Results of the Ypsilanti Perry Preschool Project. Final report*. Ypsilanti, Michigan: High / Scope Educational Research Foundation.

WEIKART, D.P., ROGERS, L., ADCOCK, C., and McCLELLAND, D. (1971). *The Cognitively Oriented Curriculum*. Washington, D.C.: ERIC / National Association for the Education of Young Children.

WESTINGHOUSE LEARNING CORPORATION / OHIO UNIVERSITY (1969). *The Impact of Head Start. An evaluation of the effects of Head Start on children's cognitive and affective development*. 2 volumes. Washington, D.C.: Office of Economic Opportunity.

WILLIAMS, G. (1970). 'Compensatory education.' In: BUTCHER, H.J. and PONT, H.B. (Eds) *Educational Research in Britain 2*. London: University of London Press.

WILLIAMS, H.L. (1973). 'Compensatory education in the nursery school.' In: CHAZAN, M. (Ed) *Compensatory Education*. London: Butterworths.

WILLIAMS, T. (1975). 'Dimensions of family environments,' *Generator of Division G of the American Educational Research Association*, 6 (1), 2—5.

WISEMAN, S. (1964). *Education and Environment*. Manchester: Manchester University Press.

WISEMAN, S. (1967). The Manchester survey. Appendix G. In: GREAT BRITAIN: DEPARTMENT OF EDUCATION AND

SCIENCE. *Children and their Primary Schools, volume 2: Research and surveys*. London: HMSO.

WISEMAN, S. (1968). 'Educational deprivation and disadvantage.' In: BUTCHER, H.J. (Ed) *Educational Research in Britain*. London: University of London Press.

WISEMAN, S. and GOLDMAN, R. (1970). 'Deprivation and disadvantage: England and Wales.' In: PASSOW, A.H. (Ed) *Deprivation and Disadvantage: Nature and manifestations*. Hamburg: UNESCO Institute for Education.

WOLF, R.M. (1966). Identification and measurement of environmental process variables related to intelligence. Unpublished PhD thesis, University of Chicago.

WOODHEAD, M. (1976). *Intervening in Disadvantage: A challenge for nursery education*. Slough: NFER.

WOODWARD, J.A. and OVERALL, J.E. (1975). 'Multivariate analysis of variance by multiple regression methods,' *Psychological Bulletin*, **82**, 21—32.

ZIGLER, E. (1966). 'Mental retardation: Current issues and approaches.' In: HOFFMAN, L.W. and HOFFMAN, M.L. (Eds) *Review of Child Development Research, volume 2*. New York: Russell Sage Foundation.

ZIGLER, E. (1970). 'Social class and the socialization process,' *Review of Educational Research*, **40**, 87—110.